PENNSYLVANIA'S UNEXPLAINED MYSTERIES

Ghosts, UFOs, Cryptids, & More

PACKANACK
publishing

"There are nights when the wolves are silent, yet the moon still howls."

CONTENTS

INTRODUCTION

I've been fascinated by ghosts and monsters for as long as I can remember. Over the years I've had countless people approach me, wanting to share their encounters with the unexplainable.

I decided it was time to give them that outlet.

This short book includes first-hand reports as told by the people who lived them. They are raw and oftentimes emotional. While they might not all be polished and professionally written, I wanted to keep the stories in their own words and authentic.

— *Tony Urban*

GHOSTS IN THE MORGUE

y Alvin Sechler
Pittsburgh

As I WRITE this story down, I'm just under four months from my 87th birthday. What I'm about to tell happened over fifty years ago. Much of the time I can't tell you what I ate for breakfast by the time supper rolls around, but I can remember every detail of what I saw just like I'm watching it all unfold on the TV. All I need to do is close my eyes and I'm right back there. In the Pittsburgh City Morgue.

I worked night security at the morgue, had since I was 25. Far as jobs went it was just okay. The hours weren't too swell as I was never a night owl, but I got used to it after four or six months.

Most nights passed without incident. Most excitement that usually came along was if some drunk wrapped his Chevy around a tree and had to be brought in. Sometimes in pieces.

Oh, there were a few times I earned my keep. Once we had a group of college kids trying to get into a fraternity. They were tasked with stealing a toe tag off one of the bodies. Part of their initiation, I guess. Two of 'em came to the door and got my attention, then told me their car had got a flat and they didn't know how to work a jack. They looked about dumb enough for that to be the truth so I followed 'em outside to lend a hand. Shoulda known better.

While I was out there, two more of 'em snuck inside. The morgue back then wasn't much of nothing far as size went. I had a little office inside the door. A desk really, with a telephone and lamp. Not an office at all I suppose. Aside from that it was just a couple a room, most for storing records. Made finding the icebox pretty simple. Alls you had to do was follow the black wheel marks over the tile floor, had yourself a road map.

Those two fellas, they made it to the

morgue. But joke was on them cuz, like I said, most nights was slow and all the dead folks, they'd already been transported to whatever funeral home they'd be getting their goodbyes in. I'd just come back inside about the time those boys realized they'd struck out, caught 'em flat footed.

See, they left the door to the morgue open and that got my attention, so I went exploring. When I stepped into the room, one of 'em screamed so shrill I wondered if he was a boy at all. Never seen folks run so fast less they was in a race. I don't know for sure, but I bet they had to change their jockey shorts when they got back to wherever it was they were going.

Then there was the time we had ourselves a four car pile up downtown. Wouldn't of been too bad except one of the vehicles involved was a limousine with five people on board, plus the driver. They ended up most of the way under a garbage truck and, well, I won't get into details, but I'll just say, we had a full house that night. More bodies than places to put 'em. By then I was used to seeing the corpses, much as you can get used to such a thing that is. Still, I preferred when they were tucked away, not sitting out in the open. The latter, that stuck me as unseemly. The dead deserve privacy, at least that's the way I came to see it.

I'm rambling though. I tend to do that and I'll apologize but that don't mean I won't do it again.

To get back to what I was saying, most nights at the morgue were quiet. I won't go as far as to say peaceful, but quiet. I spend most of the shift reading. Detective books were my vice. Dashiell Hammett, Raymond Chandler, those types of fellows. I'd even take a flyer on a Talmage Powell from time to time. I'd go through four books a week at a minimum.

In between reading, I'd make my rounds. Once around the building, then poking my nose into every room to be certain nothing was amiss. Did that every other hour, so four times a shift.

I was the only soul in the building most of the time. The only live soul, that is. Some folks - heck, maybe most folks - would think that's creepy, but I liked the peace of it. Gave my mind time to turn without voices acting as roadblocks.

A man needs quiet time. I think that's half the problem with the world today. Folks never get left alone with their thoughts. Too many telephones and computers and now they even merged the two together. Gotten to the point where a man can't even take a healthy dump without a phone in his hand.

Sorry. Like I said. Rambling.

Anyways, I'd been working the job for a few years and settled into a good routine. I got on a first name basis with most of the cops in the area. City cops, town clowns, even the stateys. Most of them were good fellows. I suppose a part of me wanted to be in their shoes. Like the detectives I read about in those stories. Solving mysteries. Doing something important. But not every man's meant to carry a burden like that. I wasn't, that's for certain.

The Pirates had just finished up a series against the Cubbies. Swept it, even. That was back when they was able to field a good team. Not like now. After the game, some fan who'd celebrated a might too hard didn't successfully navigate his way home. Ended up crashing head on with a nurse who was walking down the sidewalk on her way to the hospital. His car pinned her against a building and he went through his own windshield. Instead of him going home and her going to work, they both came to see me.

The officer who came in with the bodies, his name was Bill Halleck but everyone called him Squint because he needed glasses but rarely wore them, so he squinted his eyes down to something in the vicinity of twenty twenty. Squint gave me the paperwork and we strolled down the hall, two ambulance drivers each pushing a gurney with a body covered in a sheet.

Because of those sheets, I couldn't see the bodies, but I could tell from the outlines that it was pretty rough. Well, the outlines, and the blood. Never could understand why they used white sheets. Black woulda been a better choice, but nobody asked my opinion. Those sheets, they were just about as red as Cardinal Wright's vestment by the time they got back to the icebox. What a mess.

I signed 'em in and Squint and I chatted a spell about the ballgame and life in general. Then he got a call on his radio and was out of there. Just me and my books. And the bodies. Business as usual.

This was only half an hour or so into my shift and I had a little wait before my next rounds. That came and went as usual. Everything right as rain.

It was the second go around when things got... odd. Everything was normal outside. The inside rooms, they was all empty and ordinary. But, when I got to the icebox, both of the drawers where those folks bodies had been stored were hanging open.

I could see one door maybe not being latched on accident, but both? Seemed implausible. I walked over and gave 'em both a hard shove and made sure they were closed. Then I checked 'em again. Can never be too certain. Then I went back to my desk and my book and poured another capful of coffee outta my thermos, settling in for the next two hours.

When it came time for the next rounds, I did the usual. Outside. Inside. Always saved the icebox for last. Just as I pushed that door open, I heard a low, almost inaudible, moan.

I figured it was my stomach. It tended to grumble toward the end of shift. Hankering bacon and eggs. Maybe some sausage if the missus was feeling generous. Didn't give it much thought.

Until I stepped into the room. And, swear on my daughters, those doors were both open again. Just a crack, just like the time prior. Almost like when you close the refrigerator door too hard and it pops open a fraction of an inch. I closed 'em again. Checked 'em again. Then went back to reading.

I was in the middle of a real good chapter when I heard the scream. Startled me so much my feet, which had been propped not he desk, kicked out and knocked over my thermos. Sent a good pint of coffee all over the paperwork. I'd catch heck for that come morning, but at the time, I didn't care much.

Because that was a woman's scream and I knew there weren't any women in the building.

At least, none of the living kind.

I knew where that scream had come from. I could tell from the hollow, echo-y way it carried through the hall. It came from the morgue and that's where I headed.

We didn't have firearms back then, but even if I'd have been carrying I doubt I would've pulled it out because I was a level-headed fellow and I knew I was alone. Had to be. I'd checked twice already.

But I could still hear that scream, rolling around inside my head as I moved down the hallway. It wasn't the high, girlish scream of a young miss who'd found a spider on her bedsheets or almost stepped on a snake. It was a scream full of pain. Full of anguish. The kind of scream someone makes as they're being put out.

I was about halfway down the hall when that scream rang out again. It was so loud it almost seemed to be coming from inside my own head. I wouldn't have been surprised if my eardrums had burst, it was that loud.

I had to lean against the wall to steady myself, an act that took a good minute or more. I was just about ready to carry on when I heard a new sound. Not a scream that time, but more of a gurgle. The way it sounds to carry on a conversation underwater and the voices are thick and full and impossible to decipher. That only last a few seconds, then stopped, and I moved on.

When I got to the door to the morgue, I didn't push it straight in like I usually woulda. I waited, trying to focus my ears if such a thing's possible, trying to hear. But all I could hear was my own breathing which, let me tell you, was coming fast and hard.

But I was paid to do a job and I intended to do it. So I pushed open that door and stepped inside.

I didn't find any woman. What I did find

were those two drawer doors open again. Not just a crack either, they whole way open that time. It was like I was being invited to take a good look.

Now, I'll admit, sometimes curiosity got the better of me. I didn't peek at all the expirations that passed through the building, but I'd saw a fair percentage of them. And I was curious about all that blood on the sheets. So, I decided to have myself a look-see.

I pulled out the first drawer, the one with the fella on it. Then I pulled out the second. they weren't exactly side by side, but they were close enough. I stared at the both of them before doing anything. Before deciding what I was doing, I suppose.

The blood-soaked sheets were clinging to the bodies, which made it more obvious that something under there wasn't right. You could tell they were people, but it was like a jigsaw puzzle where a couple of pieces where in wrong, maybe forced in where they shouldn't have been.

As I reached for the sheet over the fella, I heard that gurgling, underwater sound again and snatched my hand back. Then I told myself

I was being foolish and I grabbed that sheet and jerked it to the side.

Then I saw it.

A head. But not his head.

Her head, shoulder, and left arm were placed above the man's lower half.

I pulled off the sheet on the other body and found the other misplaced parts. Whoever had gathered those poor folks up at the scene had done a piss poor job of it, that was for certain. But that wasn't my mess to clean up, so I put the sheets back over them, slid the drawers back in place, and closed 'em in.

I was almost back to the door when I felt the hand on my forearm. The skin was cold as a metal pole on a winter day and I half-expected to see my skin blister. I looked down and saw a woman's delicate fingers touching me. I could see right through them, like it was some sort of mirage. Then I saw and felt her hand close over my arm and squeeze.

Then she screamed again.

I spun around, almost slipping on that slick, tile floor, and I suppose you might guess what I found.

Both doors were open again.

Maybe I did too much reading for my own

good, but I got the feeling that this was happening for a reason. And that reason was because that woman and man wanted their pieces put back together proper.

So , that's what I did. Their bodies were just about as cold as the hand that had touched my arm, but I pushed through.

When it was finished, I closed 'em up one last time. On the next round, when I checked the morgue, their doors were closed and they stayed that way till the morning. I didn't hear any more screams, no more of that gurgling sound, which I now believe it what it must sound like when someone is choking on their own blood.

I never told the morning shift guard what happened. Never mentioned it to Squint neither. But when those ambulance boys came back the next time I gave them both an earful and told 'em to be more careful from then on when it came to putting bodies back together.

I told 'em the dead deserve respect and, if they aren't awarded it, they'll find a way to get it. One way or another.

The dead get what they want.

THE OLD FARMHOUSE

*B*y Beth Hutchinson
Friedens

IT WAS the summer of 1995 and my brothers and I were preparing for a big move as our parents decided it was time to find a bigger home for their growing family. We would leave behind our friends and the neighborhood we had grown to love and move to an old 1800's farmhouse located in wide-open fields near Friedens, Pennsylvania.

The closest neighbors at the new place were at least half a mile away. With its asphalt shingle siding, large wormy, chestnut beams, and a spring-fed trough in the basement which provided water for the home, this house would become the first place I experience my early paranormal encounters.

Dad and mom were glad for more space, and it was more affordable to rent. The deal was our family helped with the farm work and did the daily feeding of the cattle. It was a more affordable way for us to live in a larger home.

My first impression of the place was that of the old house's aura or energy. It felt different, and I couldn't explain why. It was almost as if we were not welcome or didn't belong. The feeling made no sense. I wasn't the only one feeling this because my little brother expressed the same opinion. He and I were to share a bedroom until my parents could finish carpeting the 3rd room for me.

Our first night sleeping there was terrifying. David, my little brother, woke me up in the middle of the night.

"Sis, do you hear that?" he asked. His eyes were wide and full of concern.

I sat up in the bed and listened carefully to what he may have been hearing. It didn't take long for me to catch the cause of his distress.

As I listened, it sounded a like someone was walking around on the floor above us. The sound of heavy boots trudged back and forth across the attic floor. The steps were pacing in long, slow strides.

It made no sense because everyone else was in bed, and no other person should be in the house that late at night. My heart started beating faster.

As we listened, the footsteps began descending the attic steps, coming towards the door, which was located directly across from our bedroom. Each step thumped on the wood one at a time until they reached the landing. The metal latch, which was the only thing keeping the door shut, began to shake and rattle. Soon enough, the lock lifted to release the door, and it swung open ever so gently.

David trembled in my bed, frightened at what was coming out of the attic. "Who's there?" he asked.

There was no answer. We had no idea what to expect at that point. Was there going to be someone standing there?

Just as quickly as the door opened, it swung shut, and the metal latch returned to its original place. Footsteps began their way back up the steps and into the attic. Once they reached the top of the attic steps, it stopped. There were no other sounds that night.

However, it wouldn't be the only night. The unknown footsteps occurred just the same many nights after that. Sometimes, the strange steps would be in the attic. In other instances, footsteps walked on the steps leading to the first floor and basement.

There was a morning when I was getting prepared to do the morning feeding. I dressed in my outdoor clothes and reached for the basement door when I heard walking coming up from the basement. It reached the other side of the basement door and stopped. Instead of opening the door to fetch my boots, I exited out of the front door instead. There was no reason for anyone to be in the basement as it was completely locked, and everyone else was still in bed.

Other strange things occurred as the years went by. There was a period when a small touch lamp located in my parents' bedroom would be on almost every night at around 5 PM. It was undoubtedly unsettling when we would make sure the light was turned off and discovered turned back on later when no one was around.

The most unnerving experience happened during Christmas one year. Our family dog, Little Bear, was a Pomeranian who we adopted as a pup to live with us as an indoor pet. Little Bear was sitting up on my bed, watching me as I sat on the bedroom floor with my small CD player. Christmas music played as I drew little sketches on paper. Passing the time away, this was my activity while everyone else was downstairs watching Christmas shows in the living room.

I could hear the rest of the family through the bedroom vents, which were open vents to allow heat to rise from the first floor to the second. One could easily see straight through to the lower level. It was an effective method to yell for one another when we wanted to communicate from the between levels.

As I listened to the music, a little girl was singing, "Away in the Manger" on the CD player. Everything was calm until, suddenly, the peace was disturbed by a loud *BANG, BANG, BANG!*

My heart immediately jumped out of my chest, and I quickly pressed pause on the player.

All I could hear were the loud thumps of my heartbeat in my ears.

Little Bear perked up, looking towards the bedroom door. He began growling towards the direction of the loud noise. The bangs came from the attic door. Whatever that was, it didn't like Christmas music.

Slowly, I stood up. No other sounds were coming from the attic door. As fast as I could, I ran out of the bedroom, dashed down to the first floor where the rest of the family was, with Little Bear keeping up right behind me at my heels.

Years went by, and we continued to have these paranormal experiences at random times. One evening my brother was going into the kitchen to get a drink. It was dark, and he reached over to flip the switch to turn on the overhead light. It was then he saw what appeared to be a bulky man standing in our kitchen near the sink. He claimed there were no facial features, and after a few seconds, the man vanished. This experience was undoubtedly disturbing to David, and it was the only time an apparition was seen by any of us.

My dad brought home an old upright

piano. The piano company that made this musical instrument was from "Pittsburg" (spelled without the "H" at the end during the period when Pittsburgh dropped this additional letter). The piano sat in the corner of the living room, directly underneath our bedroom.

On one particular evening, not long after we got the piano, a sound woke me up in the middle of the night. I could hear it coming from the vent leading down to the floor below. I got myself out of bed and leaned down low to listen. Everyone else was sound asleep. It did not take long before I could hear four little notes hit on the piano keys.

My eyes got wide, but it was too dark to see anything. There were no lights on down below. With no other notes played after a few minutes, I returned to bed.

As time went on, we eventually moved to a new home, and the old house sat empty for many years. An interested buyer wanted to purchase the farmhouse to tear it down and rebuild a new one at another location, using the wormy chestnut beams for a new structure. The wood was valuable and would make good wood for the style home he wanted to build. Therefore, the haunted place got dismantled and is no longer in existence. My family and I would never forget what strange things witnessed there.

Later, we researched the history of the location. Supposedly, one of the previous residents had become ill and died in the home. My family believed that the apparition my brother saw and the man who died might be the same. His spirit may potentially be the cause of all the unexplained experiences. We couldn't say for sure, but what we witnessed was very real to us.

MY DAD PROVED IT

*B*y *Gidget Brooks*
Meyersdale

I HAVE ALWAYS BEEN interested in the paranormal. In ghost Stories. In books. In horror movies that are less gory and more about, *"Hey, that could be true and could happen to me!"*

Everyone in my family enjoyed the supernatural, but some of us believed more than others. Some of us sought out those types of stories. Some of us did some research - extensive research - into the paranormal. But not my Dad.

While he thought it was fun to watch

scary movies, he thought it was all fiction. As I grew older, and my interest in the paranormal increased, my Dad would often tease me about it. He would say, *"Oh, is the boogeyman gonna get me!?"* or, when talking about psychics or supposedly true stories, *"You actually think that stuff is real? Those people saw you coming and got every penny out of you they could."*

As he got into his older years and his health started to decline, his attitude changed. One evening he, my mom, and I were sitting in the living room and he made one of the snarky remarks, he was so well known for. Then, I saw him duck his head and glance behind him. I didn't think much of it at the time.

That was until he did the same thing a few nights later. Then again one afternoon after lunch. I was curious, so the next time he did it I asked him why he kept ducking and looking over his shoulder when he made those sarcastic comments.

Dad got a serious look on his face, and also seemed confused. Maybe because he didn't want to admit believing what he was thinking. He said, *"Every now and then I will say something, and then get the feeling my mother is standing behind me and she's gonna smack me on the head for what I just said."*

I kind of chuckled and teased, *"What's this? I think you just admitted you believe in ghosts!"*

He very seriously said, *"Well, sometimes I get the feeling she's standing right behind me."*

My Grandmother and I were very close, and I remembered her admonishing us like that when she was alive. I told my Father that, maybe he should be a little nicer and he wouldn't have to worry about her smacking him on the head.

My Dad suffered from diabetes and many complications that come along with that disease. As he suffered the ravages of the illness, he began to take the subject of ghosts much more seriously. From time to time, while watching horror movies he'd mention that they scared him and that he should stop watching them. He even admitted to believing such events could be possible.

One evening, while we were watching TV, he had made one of his snarky comments, ducked, and looked back. We both chuckled and I said, "Go ahead Grandma, smack him. He deserves it for that comment."

Dad retorted with, "Well, joke if you want

to. But when I die, if ghosts are real, I'll come back and let you know." We both laughed and carried on with the evening.

A few months later, my Dad passed away.

Everything was hectic during the weeks after the funeral. My son (who was still in junior high school at the time) and I lived about 15 minutes from the farm I grew up on, and where my mother still lived. One day, when I had come home from work, I went to unlock the front door to enter and realized it was already unlocked.

My son always went straight from school to football practice, so I knew he hadn't been home yet. He had left after me that morning, so I was a bit annoyed, assuming he'd forgotten to lock the door on his way out.

When he got home, I lectured him about being responsible. He apologized, but insisted he'd locked it. A few days later, I came home and the door was again unlocked. I once more scolded my son, and he again insisted he'd locked it. This happened a few more times until one day, when I came home, the door was standing wide open.

I was beyond annoyed. This child had always been a responsible kid. Being the son of a single parent, he had to take on more responsibility than many of his friends, and he'd always handled it well. I knew he was upset when his Grandpa passed, but it didn't seem like something that would make him forgetful enough to lock the house and I began to wonder why he was acting this way.

When he returned from practice, my patience had reached its end. I told him that leaving the door unlocked was bad enough, but leaving the door hanging open was completely unacceptable.

He said, *"Mom, I was running late and had a friend pick me up for school. When I got in the car, I said, 'Wait, I have to go back and check the door. Mom keeps accusing me of leaving it open.'"*

He promised that he'd gone back to the house and verified the door was locked. And I believed him. The only other possibility I could come up with was that our neighbor, who had had a key for emergencies, had gone inside for some reason. I called to check, and of course, the neighbor said they hadn't unlocked or opened our door. Nothing was missing or out of place and there were no signs anyone had entered the house

One day, while discussing this with my mom, she jokingly said, *"Maybe it is your Dad letting you know it is true. Ghosts are real."*

Her comment kept running through my mind and I began to think it might be possible. I told myself that, if it happened again, I'd know it was dad reaching out, just like he'd promised.

Sure enough, the next day the door was again standing wide open. I went inside, closed the door, and said loudly, "Ok Dad, I understand now. It is true! But quit opening my door or someone is going to rob us!"

The door was never unlocked again.

Of course, my young teenage son never stopped reminding me that I'd wrongly accused him and that, sometimes, there are other explanations. When he does that, his tone is a bit snarky, just the way his Grandfather would have said it.

SOMETHING IN THE WOODS

*A*nonymous
Central PA

IT WAS a late September evening around 2006 and I was working as a Deputy Wildlife Conservation Officer with the Pennsylvania Game Commission. My partner and I were patrolling a somewhat remote location in Central PA. The area is many thousands of wooded acres separated only by the occasional hard road. One particular spot was known to be a popular weekend party destination for local teens, so we regularly checked to ensure nothing objectionable or illegal was going on.

We arrived in the general area around 1 a.m and decided to park several hundred yards away and walk in. This allowed us to discreetly enter areas without alerting people and giving them a chance to flee. We walked down a small dirt road to where a stone fire ring was located in a little basin surrounded on one side by hardwoods and scattered brush, and pines on the other.

While at the fire ring, everything was very quiet and there was no sign of teenagers. But, as we surveyed the area, we heard a noise through the pine trees. Thinking it may be someone on their way in, we waited to see who might show up. As the noise got closer, we could tell it was something walking, but something too heavy to be a person. As Conservation Officers, our first thought was - a bear.

When it was about 100 yards out, it started breaking branches and limbs as it came closer. It was making too much noise to be a bear - or at least one of normal size. Realizing this was not anything we normally had to deal with, we started to walk carefully back towards our vehicle.

At one point, whatever was making the

noise was close enough that we thought it had to be only a few feet inside the concealment of the pines, just out of our sight. Our flashlights revealed nothing, but we knew it was close and getting closer. We drew our handguns fully expecting whatever it was to make a rush for us, but nothing charged.

We continued to walk back to the truck, never turning our backs on the noise. The steps, the crunching, the breaking branches, all those sounds trailed us as we retreated, but there was something new added in.

Aggressive, low growls.

Finally we were at our vehicle, and were never so happy to jump into that truck. Flicking on the headlights revealed nothing, so we threw it in reverse and got out of there.

After calling predators for over 25 years, and spending 18 years in wildlife law enforcement, I have never experienced anything else like that. I had heard something that sounded like what some call "wood knocks" before, including in the same general area where we heard the growls, but after that night, I never went back.

To this day, I don't know what it WAS, but

despite spending so much of my life in the woods, I know it was like nothing I had encountered before, and hopefully never encounter again.

HAUNTING ON EDISON STREET

*B*y *Adam Gmutza*
Uniontown Area

IN THE LATE summer of 2004, my siblings and I all found ourselves having experiences with a dark entity within our childhood home in Uniontown, Pennsylvania. It all seemed to begin when my sister and her boyfriend decided to purchase a foreclosed home in New Kensington, Pennsylvania in order to renovate to sell.

They thought it was a dream come true when the 100+ year old, three story Victorian came onto the market. Even with the rough exterior they could see the potential in the beautiful house with the stained glass windows still intact, and decided to purchase it.

They were later informed by a neighbor that the house had a dark history. While it sat abandoned for many years there were squatters, drug abuse, prostitution, and even instances of satanic rituals.

While renovating the nearly gutted home my sister and her boyfriend came across some abandoned objects including a photo album, a strange-looking pendant consisting of two snakes wrapped around an apple that opened into a locket, and a portrait of a husband and wife.

The latter had a sinister feel. The man and the women bore emotionless expressions and seemed almost dead behind the eyes. Looking into this portrait left the viewer with an uneasy, uncomfortable feeling.

My siblings and I, although disturbed by these objects and despite the sordid history of the house, felt intrigued by them. We decided to keep them and brought them back to our home. That's when our experiences began.

At first it seemed playful, like pranks. One such instance was when my sister Sara seemed to have misplaced her wallet. After tearing the whole living room apart, moving chairs, flipping couches, and searching high and low, we admitted defeat and called off our search.

Days later, Sara and I were sitting on the living room floor when, out of nowhere, she caught something out of the corner of her eye. There, in plain sight, was the wallet, lying in the middle of the floor. There seemed to be no explanation for how the both of us had missed the wallet during our previous search and in the days leading up to its discovery.

It was in that same room where the entity that haunted us made its first appearance. Early on a Friday evening, I was entering the house through the back door, which opened into the kitchen. While standing parallel with the threshold, I could see into the living room. There, sitting in the living room was a dark shadow of a man.

The man wasn't transparent, but would better be described as a dark, smokey blur. The only defining features were his height and face. He looked to have been over 6 feet tall and had dark, hollow depressions where his eyes should have been.

The whole face looked like that of a skeleton, with high cheekbones and a sunken in look. The bottom jaw seemed to be missing. He was expressionless, emotionless. Lifeless.

As I watched, the man leaned to the side and peered through the door frame, looking directly at me. Frozen and unable to move, I watched as the man stood and moved out of my line of sight. As he moved away, he slowly faded into nothingness. The fear that hit me kept me frozen in place, just staring into the living room, until my body finally regained the energy to move.

I backed out of the house, feeling panicked and afraid of being that I'd be made fun of or

mocked for what I had seen that I convinced myself that I could never tell anyone what I'd experienced that day.

A week passed and I'd kept my silence, but began to doubt myself and wondered if I was losing my mind. Then, one day I came home from school only to find my sister Sara acting unusually. We had a good relationship and she always talked and joked around with me, but when something really bothered her she would turn quiet. And she was quiet that day.

I asked her if something was wrong and Sara explained to me that she hadn't been feeling well earlier in the day and had laid down on the living room couch to watch TV and take a nap. As she was sleeping, a noise had startled her and she woke up. But her body wasn't fully awake yet.

When Sara opened her eyes the television appeared to be on a static frequency, but she couldn't hear the noise of the static that usually accompanied that. She blinked her eyes a few times, trying to chase away the lingering tiredness, but when she reopened her eyes, she spotted a dark figure passing in front of her.

Terrified, she tried to scream, but wasn't able to make a sound. She closed her eyes again only that time felt someone or something running fingers through her hair. Somehow she summoned the courage to open her eyes, only to see a dark face inches away from her own. A face

with even darker depressions where the eyes should've been.

Sara felt like she couldn't breath, as if a large weight was sitting on her chest. Out of complete fear she closed her eyes tightly and, when she opened them, the figure was gone and she could breathe again.

Hearing this story completely alarmed me as I had told not one person about what I had seen and from how Sara described what she just witnessed, there was no doubt it was the same figure I saw a week earlier. I told Sara what I'd seen and she couldn't believe that we had had two different experiences but saw the very same dark menacing face.

The sightings started becoming a normal routine for a few weeks. My oldest sister Erin experienced this figure when she was on the computer doing some work when she noticed something from her peripheral vision. When she glanced over she saw, what she described, as an elderly man missing the bottom half of his jaw walk through the kitchen and disappear.

After this, the figure itself seemed to only want to show itself in the kitchen. Once, Sara was home all by herself preparing a meal when she caught the reflection of a figure rushing up behind her. Afraid that someone had broken into our home she turned around immediately to face the assailant, but only found an empty kitchen.

As Erin, Sara, and myself discussed these strange and terrifying occurrences, we came to the conclusion that we had to get rid of every item we brought into our home from the New

Kensington house. Since removing the items, the activity has stopped completely.

I am convinced that the tall, dark figure of a man that haunted us for months was the very same person from the photo in the locket and that he was not happy with us removing it from the house. Even though the activity has stopped, when I go in the house, sometimes I still feel like I'm being watched.

GHOSTLY GETTYSBURG GIRLS TRIP

y Julie Koval
Gettysburg

ON SEPTEMBER 30TH 2007 three girlfriends & I decided to take a trip to Gettysburg for some relaxation and ghost hunting. Not exactly what you think of when you picture a girls trip, but we always liked to do something different.

We stayed at the Cashtown Inn, and had several experiences during our three day stay. The most memorable for myself, was our first night in town. In the fall, you can be on the battle grounds for some time after dark, because of the time change. I was with one of my friends that night and we decided to investigate the wheat field.

We pulled over along the side of the road, and walked maybe a quarter of the way into the field before stopping as it was very dark with heavy clouds obscuring the moon. My friend had set up a small cassette player boom box, and started to play the song "I Wish I Was In Dixie." She was a much more avid ghost hunter than I at the time, and I must admit, I was quite amused!

She then explained that this concept could bring the spirits near! By this time in my life, I had been to a few investigations and I had learned to take pictures by listening to my five senses for direction.

We stood, alone in the dark, in the middle of this grown up wheat field, for at least 30 minutes. We were just taking in the night, playing "Dixie" and thinking of the battle that happened all around us during the Civil war.

I started to take pictures with my film camera about 15 minutes in. At one point, when I turned my camera to the right and away from where my friend was standing, I felt the hair raise up on my neck. Feeling like something was up, I began to snap photos in that direction. A few minutes later, the funny feeling left, and soon after, we decided to pack it in and go explore another area of the battle field.

When we got home I sent the film off to be developed and within a week I had my photos back. There were several taken in the wheat field that had a strange, misty-like apparition. It had circle orbs of light shooting out from it and looked like a man laying on the ground with his head covered by a blanket. As I thought about it, it made sense that a mortally wounded man, bleeding out, as he lay dying would be cold. He would be trying to stay warm, even in the hot summer heat.

Fast forward to two years after that girls trip. I took my daughter to Gettysburg. It was July 20th 2009 & we learned about a soldier who was killed in battle at the wheat field! This is an account from that very day, during the battle.

Gettysburg - The wheat field and Peach Orchard - July 2, 1863.

Around 6:00 p.m., as the Union position around the Peach Orchard collapsed, the V Corps brigades of Sweitzer and Tilton fell back from the Wheat field. However, the II Corps division of General John Caldwell soon arrived from Cemetery Ridge to take their place. The brigades of Edward Cross, Patrick Kelly and Samuel Zook deployed left to right across the field and on the stony hill to the west. The brigade of John Brooke was in support. Cross's brigade guided on a stone wall on the east edge of the field, where Cross was killed leading his old 5th New Hampshire regiment.

As soon as I saw his name, it all seemed to connect in my mind. This was the apparition man laying in the field that night in September 2007. I believe the figure in my photos is Edward Cross's ghost.

GRANDMA'S HOUSE

*B*y *Deborah Vick*
Johnstown

I GREW up in my grandparents house at the corner of Union and Locust streets in downtown Johnstown. It was an old house, small and far from grand, built in the early 1900's. One wall was actually shared with the house next door, a home built by my great-great grandparents after the 1889 Johnstown flood. If you were brave enough to venture into the attic you could still see one of the original windows from the other house that wasn't covered on our side.

In the 14 years I lived there, I might have

ventured into that attic two or three times at the most. I know... attics are always the settings for ghost stories... but it really did creep me out. The unlit hallway was equally scary and I'd recite the Lord's Prayer every time I had to pass the attic door to get to my bedroom. In some ways, I always felt kind of spooked anywhere in that house... just that feeling like you were never quite alone.

Since the house was so small, I shared a bedroom with my grandmother and aunt. One warm summer night, when I was about 10 years old, I had fallen asleep reading. Due to the heat, the windows were open to let in fresh air, and I was awakened by chatter and traffic when the night's game at Point Stadium let out.

The noise had me wide awake but I couldn't go back to reading because they shut off the big stadium lights that shone in the window and provided my reading light, so I just laid there with my back to the bedroom door and hoped to fall back to sleep. Soon thereafter, I began to get this weird feeling, like someone was behind me, like someone was there, but I hadn't heard anyone come in.

I started getting really scared and was trying to work up enough courage to turn around and look. That seemed to take forever, but when I finally got brave enough, I turned around to see a swirling mist slowly coming toward me. I could sort of see an image, but it was moving and trying to form into something but not quite making it.

I was absolutely terrified. I couldn't move. My mouth was open, trying to scream, but I couldn't. All of a sudden my aunt woke up and turned the lamp on and headed downstairs for a drink of water. Whatever was there dissolved away and, as it did, I finally managed to start screaming. I was hysterical and it took awhile for me to settle down.

My aunt said she didn't see a thing and they all tried to tell me I was dreaming. I argued that I wasn't asleep. I know I was wide awake. I'd heard the people coming from the ballgame and my neighbor talking and clanking her dishes, all the typical sounds of the neighborhood. I know what I saw and to this day I can still see it in my mind.

Needless to say, I wouldn't go upstairs at night by myself after that and wasn't really keen on going up there in daylight either. I don't know who or what I saw, or if it was good or evil. I just know it darn near scared the life out of me.

I've thought about it from time to time since. I was the 5th generation to live on that land. Lots of family had lived and died there and were even laid out in our parlor. Maybe it was my 3x great grandmother who lived on that land when the 1889 flood waters struck and swept her to her death, or maybe it was some other lost soul. I'll never know and I'm not sure I want to know.

Several years later my grandmother was living in a nursing home and my mom passed away. I went to live in a children's home until I graduated high school in 1967. When I came back, the houses were torn down and replaced by a parking lot. I do wonder what became of my visitor and all the others who made me feel like I was never quite alone in that house. Maybe they moved to a neighbor's house or stayed in the parking lot and caught a ride home with someone after work. Wherever they went, I hope they found peace.

LIGHT FROM ABOVE

*A*nonymous
Jennerstown

IN THE SPRING of 2013 I visited some friends for a meal and a movie. It was a fun evening and I always enjoyed getting out of the house after my husband's sudden passing the year prior.

Around eleven p.m. we called it a night. I had a short drive home, about six miles. I live in a rural area and there was no other traffic on the two-lane that time of night, so I expected a quick, uneventful trip. I've never been so wrong.

I was less than a mile from the home of my

friends' when, out of nowhere, night seemingly turned to day. The sudden illumination came from directly above me and the light was so directional that I could see the hard shadows created as it crossed my car.

It was so bright that everything inside my car was lit up too. I had to squint just to be able to see because it was nearly blinding.

There were no cars coming toward me. I checked my mirrors and there were none behind me. Yet this light continued.

The illumination was focused on my car and moved along, matching my speed. It was like there was something above me, shining a spot light onto my little Ford sedan.

I slowed to stop, rolled down my window, and looked into the sky. Even though the sun had set hours earlier, it felt like I was staring straight into the sun. I couldn't make out anything but light.

There were no sounds. No whirring of a helicopter or anything that could explain this light. The night was deathly quiet and I suddenly felt sick to my stomach with fear.

I rolled up my window and locked my doors. I accelerated, faster than I ever drove before. But as soon as I was moving again, so was the light. I was now halfway into my drive home and shaking so bad I thought I might wreck.

I began to cry as the confusion and fear overwhelmed me. I wanted off the road, away from that light, but all the businesses were closed and there was no where to go except home.

So, I drove on.

About half a mile from my home, as suddenly as the light appeared, it vanished. It was like someone had (no pun) flipped off a light switch.

Everything was so dark again so fast that I strained to see, yet I didn't dare risk slowing down or stopping. I just wanted inside my house. I wanted locked in where I could feel safe again.

I soon made it, speeding into the garage and closing the door. I sobbed for some minutes before making it into the house. I then called my friends and told them what had happened to me. To my shock and horror, they said it had been almost half an hour since I'd left their house.

How did that short, six mile drive take me nearly thirty minutes? To this day, I can't explain it. I wish I could forget it ever happened, but that's impossible. I'll forever wonder what happened on that ordinary, spring night when a light from above changed my life.

GHOST SOLDIER

*B*y Chris Geiger
Gettysburg

On a hot July morning in 2014 my wife and I arrived in Gettysburg excited to do a paranormal investigation. Our first stop was the Triangular Field. We had heard there was a lot of paranormal activity in this area including batteries being drained from cameras, voice recorders, and reports of people seeing soldiers walking through the field.

After parking in the Devil's Den parking lot we proceeded to the Triangular Field and immediately felt an electricity and heard a buzzing in the air surrounding us. We both looked at each other in disbelief and took this as a positive sign, hopeful we would be able to document something paranormal. As we walked down the path we both heard what could only be described as Civil War music drifting in from far off in the distance. We stopped to listen to it while I snapped several pictures.

I decided to try to take advantage of this energy by trying the technique of provoking any potential spirits or ghosts in the field to show themselves or make their presence known. Brigades from Texas, Alabama, Georgia and Arkansas fought at the bottom of the field while artillery guns from New York and soldiers from Pennsylvania, Maine and Indiana fired upon them. As we walked down the dirt path I mentioned the states of Texas and Alabama and asked what it was like to get blown apart from cannon fire.

We reached the bottom of the field where I continued to provoke hoping to elicit a response. I took several more pictures and we continued on the path back up the hill in the opposite direction. Halfway up we realized it was a dead end and we would have to turn back.

I'd heard that ghosts sometimes follow people, so I quickly spun around to snap a picture in hopes of catching something on my camera. As I snapped the picture my wife screamed.

When I turned to her to see what was the matter, I saw her breathing heavily with a look of fear in her eyes. I asked her what was wrong and she told me she felt something fly over her head and it knocked her sunglasses off her baseball cap. I looked and found her sunglasses on the path about five feet in front of her. She insisted that they hadn't simply fallen off, that they fit tightly on her hat, and she was so scared she wanted to leave immediately.

I was full of excitement and told her I wanted to return to the car to grab our camcorder so we could continue to document these events. She didn't want to stay, but eventually I convinced her. It took us about ten minutes to reach the parking lot, grab the camcorder and extra batteries and walk back to the Triangular Field.

When we stepped through the gate, the "electricity" in the air was gone and the field was completely silent - no more buzzing. It was like someone had "flipped a switch." I turned on the camcorder and began walking down the path while my wife stayed behind at the entrance to the field. It became obvious to me that whatever had happened was over and we weren't going to capture anything paranormal so I soon stopped filming and we returned to the car.

My wife eventually calmed down and we drove to our next destination with renewed energy. That was our only experience of the day, but we both have no doubts that there are paranormal happenings in Gettysburg and that soldiers still roam the fields.

YODER HILL HAUNTING

y Deborah Volk
Johnstown

I WOULD QUALIFY GROWING up on Yoder Hill in Johnstown City as typical. In some aspects, maybe ideal. I was within walking distance of my grandparents' home, a brisk uphill climb through a neighboring property put me right in their back yard. Purchased in the early 1950s on the salary of a steel worker, the sad, gray asbestos sided duplex was situated in the middle of Yoder Street.

My mother was roughly the age of 10, the oldest of three, when they moved in. It's hard to imagine what a day in their life was like, five of them cramped into such small living quarters with only two bedrooms, all the children sharing one. The only bathroom was inconveniently located on the basement level.

The other side of the duplex was occupied by my Grandma's brother, who was also busy raising three children. The duplex was in sorry repair, but as years advanced shingles were replaced and porches were added. By the 1970's, when I first laid eyes on it, the duplex was a renovated, tidy little home.

I began exploring Yoder Street independently with neighborhood kids around the age of 12. The street dead ends in the 600 block with a halfhearted cul-de-sac, that's where the woods begin. Myself and neighborhood kids often trekked a well-worn path that was laid down years before our feet ever touched it.

Narrow, with thick brush on either side, the path meandered through mature trees whose canopies obliterated any daylight. To the right, the ground sloped steeply downward never leveling off as far as the eye could see. It's no wonder that this hillside is the site for

Johnstown's Inclined Plane. Also once thriving on this hillside, was the Rolling Mill Coal Mine. It operated from the mid 1800s to the 1930s. A well-documented explosion in 1902 took the lives of 112 miners, one of the deadliest accidents in US mining history.

On the opposite end of Yoder Street is a small intersection that will place you on Millcreek Road. An old, winding, steep lane that leads to one of the oldest cemeteries in Johnstown, Grand View. Many of the miners from the 1902 tragedy were laid to rest there. Another frequent walking journey of ours was in the wooded area off of Millcreek. Hidden by decades old brush and towering trees was the "old road" that led processions into the back end of the cemetery. Abandoned and forgotten once Menoher Highway was built, all that remained was a crumbling brick lane and dilapidated stone pillars.

With a graveyard on one end and a horrific tragedy occurring on the other, I suppose Yoder Street could be the setting for many a ghost story, so I'll tell you mine. It begins with a tale of horrific murder that happened during the summer of 1935.

Living in the duplex on the opposite side of where my grandparents would be eventual residents was a young man named Jacob Gable. At the age of 19, he was choosing to start his adult life the hard way, by being a thief.

Around the end of May, Jacob robbed a confectionery store and was spotted leaving with the cash box under his arm. His neighbor, the elderly Mrs. Harriet Goltstein eyed him. She spoke with him several days later and insisted that he return the money or she would turn him into the authorities. This did not sit well with young Jacob, he was quoted as saying, "I decided to kill her that day but lost my nerve." So he waited, until June 17.

Mr. Gable crossed the street to Mrs. Goltstein's two story, wood framed farm house. He watched her through a window as she washed dishes. When he saw his opportunity, he entered the home knocking her down with one strike. He pounced on her, at first trying to suffocate the elderly, helpless woman. He snatched up a marble doorstop that was sitting nearby, he swung it mercilessly at her face breaking her upper jaw.

His attack continued as he found a paring

knife in the kitchen. He stabbed at her, puncturing her lung and slashing her stomach. When he was certain she was dead, he robbed the home and returned across the street to the duplex.

It was two days later when Mrs. Golstein's daughter found her body, dead at age 79. Police questioned young Jacob and he confessed his evil action when they confronted him with evidence of the robbery and the discovery of the bloody belt he wore while he bludgeoned his neighbor. He would be found guilty in September and sentenced to death the following spring. During that hearing his only question was, would the date of his execution coincide with his upcoming plans to play pinochle.

On January 4, 1937 Jacob smiled as he walked in a composed manner to the electric chair. He was pronounced dead just after midnight at Rockview Penitentiary. His body was placed in St. Joseph's Cemetery in Richland, but I think his soul stayed behind, in the duplex on Yoder Street.

My mother recalled that, when she was young, she was aware of a dark presence in their home. There was a constant feeling of heaviness, and of being watched. My aunt agreed that she always felt there were eyes on her. She said that there were many times when she would be in her bedroom dressing, she would just stare at the attic door, waiting for something to appear. She always got dressed quickly.

She remembered another incident that occurred while she slept. The three siblings shared one room, my aunt and mother shared one bed. Someone or something pulled her toes causing her to wake abruptly. In the dim light she could see my mom next to her and her brother across the room sleeping soundly. She peered intently into the adjoining room and could tell both her parents were in their bed, asleep.

She said from that night on she never slept with any of her limbs outside the blankets. She was convinced there was a monster under the bed. All of the children would run up the stairs from the bathroom located in the basement no matter the time of day. There was a constant feeling of something being just behind them, reaching for them, a constant feeling of fear. My mother and her little brother were both being plagued by nightmares. Both of them woke frequently, screaming out in their sleep.

My grandmother recalled seeing a dark mass form and move about their home on several occasions. There was no one to consult about this in the mid 1950s. Whoever she would tell would surely think she had gone insane. She had been raised by a strong Christian mother though, and she understood she was dealing with something sinister and not of our world. They were being tormented by an unseen dark force, a feeling of helplessness was setting in.

Out of sheer desperation, my grandmother took action doing the only thing that made sense to her. She went from room to room screaming at this entity to "Get out of my house." She yelled over and over, "Get Out! In the name of Jesus get out!" Grandma continued her unrelenting commands until she saw a black mass form one more time, pass through a wall and out of her home.

She said there was an almost immediate shift in the way the home felt, like a huge weight had been lifted off of the house. Whatever it was, my grandmother forced it out. Could it have been the spirit of that young murderer? Or, could it have been something older that possessed the ground that this building was set upon? Could it have been the influence in Jacob Gable's life that caused him to commit that horrendous crime?

I can't say, but what I have been told is that it has come back.

MY BIGFOOT ENCOUNTER

*B*y *Dave Groves*
Forest County

MY ENCOUNTER HAPPENED in early June of 2010. I took a friend to the Marienville/Timberline ATV trails northeast of Marienville, Pennsylvania in the Allegheny National Forest, to ride ATV's for the day. Allegheny National Forest covers approximately 515,000 acres or 800 square miles of protected wilderness in North West Pa. The forest is pretty dense in most spots and has many types of terrain. From my understanding, the Allegheny National Forest is one of the least densely populated areas east of the Mississippi River. Surrounding the Forest are more woodlands and farm country.

The two trail systems we were riding that weekend join together and make an approximate 60-80 mile loop from the northern end down to the bottom, and then back up the other side of the loop. My encounter happened on our return back up, heading North. I remember it rained very hard the night before and through the early morning because my friend, who was new to ATV'ing, didn't bring rain gear. We had to go into town to buy him some cheap rain gear and then headed up to the trail.

It rained the first half hour or so of our ride and I remember the sun coming out and it was turning into a really nice day for a ride. For those that ride ATV's, they know that the rain makes mud, which is much more fun to ride in than dust. A few hours into the ride, having stopped and observed some beaver dams, some very old oil wells, a couple logged out areas where you could see for what seemed like miles, and other cool sites that the forest has to offer, I was getting in more of a hurry to get back - it was approaching the end of the day. My buddy was way behind me so I decided to stop on the trail and wait for him. I usually don't separate from ATV buddies when riding, but this part of the trail was an abandoned logging trail and pretty easy, so I rode ahead awhile and then decided to stop and wait for him. He didn't ride fast or dangerous; he "putted" so I knew he was safe, just slow. If he didn't show up I would turn around and meet up with him.

I wasn't sitting long, In fact I've just taken off my helmet when I noticed rocks kept hitting the front right side of my ATV. They weren't large, maybe about palm-sized. It took a minute or so before it occurred to me that I was stopped and that rocks should not be flying through the air and hitting my atv. I was turning my head towards the right to follow the path of these "air rocks" as I called them, when I stopped.

I noticed a "stump" which turned out to be a dark figure, approximately 70-90 feet away, that appeared to be in a sitting or crouching in a low position. Then, as I watched, it stood upright. I'll never forget how it seemed to pop up like it was on a spring, with very little effort.

Initially I looked at its hands because I was interested to see what, if anything, it held. It was much taller than a normal human – best guess at this point would be 7.5 feet or so, and absolutely NOT a bear.

It was VERY broad at the shoulders. Almost freakishly broad – I remember that very well. It was on two legs and it was all very dark black – a shiny black – from head to toe, or as far as I could see to its feet as it was standing in 1-2 foot tall grass or taller.

As my eyes made their way up on the creature I could see its head was all black as well. There was no white or lighter color that stood out, like most animals would have on their face. I could not see clear details of the face, but it did not appear to have hair on all of its face. It appeared to be black skin - the same color black as its hair, but I could tell it wasn't hair in some spots. I noticed that the eyes were black, or very dark and deep set, with a pronounced brow ridge.

The hair was short to medium length and not shaggy. I'd say the hair was an average of 3 to 5 inches long, shorter at the head. It was almost groomed in appearance but I think it's from the hair being short and thick. At least that was my impression.

Almost as soon as my eyes were at its head

and face and I was trying to "zoom in" and get a better look at the face, it began to leave. It didn't turn and walk away, but rather it stepped straight backwards into the brush and the trees, never taking its eyes off me.

This all happened in the span of no more than 30 seconds, from the time I noticed the rocks hitting my ATV, up until it moved backwards. When I play it over and over in my mind, it seems more like 30 minutes. At that point an overwhelming fear just filled my mind, and I remember feeling like I shouldn't be in that spot any longer

I don't remember shaking in fear or anything like that, but I felt warm and almost like I was going to puke. So I hit the gas and took off. I wish now that I wouldn't have just fled, but the feeling that came over me was not like I'd experienced before. I had my smart phone/camera in my fender bag and it NEVER occurred to me to get it out and start video. I honestly couldn't move for a short period of time.

In the past, I've been surprised by people walking up on me in the woods and I've hunted all my life, so animal encounters, even bear from a distance - do not scare or alarm me. I was in the military for 6 years, and actually had the honor to serve as SEAL TEAM 4 and SDV TEAM 2 (the old UDT TEAM 2) support, as part of a special warfare boat crew. During that time, I had many highly anxious experiences as one could imagine. I'm pretty observant, I don't have a tendency to overreact, and I don't scare easily. I am very level headed and definitely not crazy.

I didn't instantly think "Bigfoot" as I wasn't a REAL believer then. This encounter took my emotions to places they had not been or at least had not been for a long time. It has been going through my head for over 4 years. I didn't tell anybody except my fiancée within the first year after the encounter.

Now - quite a few people know. The person I was riding with that day just found out in 2014. I never told him about the story before, but because I couldn't remember if it was springtime/early summer or late summer/Fall when this happened. I asked him what week if he remembered. When he told me it was springtime / early summer, he naturally asked why – what's up? I told him what happened. It turns out that he believes in these creatures too.

He then realized why I was acting so weird when we finally caught back up with each other, and then on the 2 and a half hour truck ride home. Now I wish I would have told him then. Maybe we could have joined together and gone back to look for signs or whatever we could find. Instead, the overwhelming feeling of "What the heck was that", and "I can't tell anybody-they won't believe me anyways" took over, and I kept it to myself.

Nobody has to tell me what I saw or didn't see. I knew what I saw. I saw a large dark figure with hair that could throw rocks (and very accurately), stand up within 100 feet from me, in a large dense forest where there aren't any cabins or people just hanging out. I still do leave the option open for an extremely large man (larger than anyone I have ever met) in a heavily padded Gillie suit with hair on it standing about 100 foot from the trail just waiting for someone to stop in that exact spot so he could throw rocks at him and take a chance of getting shot (most folks on ATVs will pack a handgun when riding in deep woods. At least that's my experience).

Now that's being sarcastic, but trying to make a truth out of what happened. Of course that option is slim, but it will always be there as I didn't walk up to this thing and shake its hand or hug it, so being 100% sure it was a Sasquatch just isn't possible. I am at 99.999% sure though. I do know that a fear like I've not felt in a long time, if ever, took over me for awhile. Something told me to go, to move on, that I shouldn't be here right now. Again - I am a very rational person and this just didn't make sense to me at all.

I eventually plan on returning to that general area, on ATV and parking the bike and doing some walking. I just need to look around and feel comfortable with that. Ever since my encounter, I cannot put this down. I've been researching since and came across various online groups that discuss encounters. I want to learn as much as I can before returning and looking around and I want to go armed with more knowledge than I have now.

THE BROKEN VASE

 nonymous
Bedford

A FEW YEARS ago my son and I rented a log cabin for a brief, two-night getaway. The beautiful, old-fashioned cabin was built in the mid 1800s and was of the original style, with heavy chinking between the logs. The interior was rustic but charming. It was the perfect place for a break from day to day life.

Nestled in a wooded meadow, the cabin was miles from the nearest town and there were no neighbors in sight. Our first day in the cabin was uneventful. We lounged about watching movies on the small TV, strolled the grounds, picked raspberries by the pond. Our two dogs ran and played and were exhausted by day's end.

That night we experienced severe thunderstorms. The power flickered and rain battered the tin roof and leaded windows. It bordered on ominous as we had no cell reception and the driveway was dirt and rock, lined with trees. It was easy to picture one of those sprawling pines falling and blocking us in, with no way to call for assistance.

The storm, as always, passed and we listened to the soft patter of raindrops on the roof as we drifted to sleep.

The following day brought more of the same, minus the storm. We stayed up pretty late, trying to make the most of our time away, and didn't turn in until about one in the morning.

The bedrooms were on the second floor and the steps leading to them were too steep for our dogs to handle. I myself was wary of navigating them, so I slept on the couch downstairs.

After a day in the fresh air, I was exhausted and asleep almost as soon as my head hit the pillow. Then, around three a.m., I was woken by a thunderous crash.

Startled awake, in the pitch black night, I didn't know what was happening. It sounded like one of the windows had been smashed in. One of the dogs was in a crate while the other, much older fellow, was asleep on the couch with me. Neither dog made a peep despite the commotion.

I fumbled for a light and, about that same time, my son arrived. He too had heard the crash - it was impossible to miss or sleep through. We hit the lights and found the source of the noise.

A large, ceramic vase had fallen and shattered against the hardwood floor. The vase had been located on the opposite side of the room from which we'd been spending time, and had set on a sturdy end table with an upraised lip around the edges. The way the stand was built, the vase could not have been perched on the edge or set there precariously.

There was no breeze in the house, and even if there was, this was a big, heavy vase. I'd estimate it weighed nearly ten pounds. There was no logical explanation for what could have caused it to fall from that stand.

All we could determine was that something we couldn't see knocked it off.

For the next half hour, our older dog stared at that spot, not takings his eyes off it, as if he sensed something there. Later, when we'd both settled down and tried to again find sleep, I turned on my mp3 player and pressed for the music to play in random. The first song that played was Adele's *Hello* with lyrics like, "Hello, can you hear me?" and, "Hello from the other side."

It's easy to write that off as a coincidence, but as soon as the song stopped playing, it started back up again. Any other time the mp3 player cycled through the entire play list, never repeating a tune until every song on the 100+ song list had been played once. Until that night and that particular song.

Nothing unusual happened the next morning, which was also our check out day. We've always hoped to return, but so far haven't had the chance. Maybe some day, we'll find out who was trying to say, "Hello."

MOUNTAIN MYSTERY

*B*y Rev. Ron "Liomsa" Latevola
Snake Spring

MAY, 2015 was a long month of waiting as it marked my 62nd birthday and retirement. My wife and I had agreed to relocate out of the city of Altoona, PA. Our desire was for a quiet, peaceful, climate-friendly locale somewhere, anywhere in the country.

We researched at length and could not find paradise as it seems every location has its positives and negatives. However, we explored an internet ad that provided more pluses than negatives and it was just 45 miles away.

Snake Spring, PA provided such a spot. It is

a modest, private area in a valley between Tussey Mountain to the East and Evitts Mountain to the West, next to a cornfield, yet five minutes from retail necessities and medical providers. A 14 mile trip in either direction will take you to further amenities. Snake Spring Township, covering 26 square miles, was settled in 1763, has a population of 552 and is home to 550 households.

We moved in that July and all was great. Quiet, private, secluded, but, convenient to all of life's necessities. Time flew by for the remainder of that summer. Fall quickly arrived. The corn was harvested leaving an open field. The mountainside trees changed their colors brilliantly that fall before drifting to the mountain ground below, becoming bedding for the deer.

Being new to country life, all the sights and sounds were jaw-dropping and eye-opening. The camera was kept busy. One fall photo session resulted in two pictures taken to highlight the pockets of fog on the mountain. Upon downloading the pics to the desktop computer, I sat back to view and decide if any were worthy of posting on social media.

After visually scanning through them, I

narrowed them down by deleting repeats and poor quality photos. Then, something caught my eye.

I enlarged the photo multiple times. What I saw, or thought I saw, was still there. I called my wife over to the computer to confirm my eyes weren't playing tricks on me.

She saw the same thing as I did. In one photo, there was a large column to the left of the fog and the right of the utility trail. It has definitive edges, not cloudy or foggy. I was certain there wasn't a physical structure, there but I got up and walked outside anyway. I strolled toward the mountain through the stubs of corn stalks in the field. I viewed the mountainside and nope, not one structure of any kind was anywhere near the vicinity of the column in the photo. A mystery indeed. A portal perhaps?

Here is an added twist. We own, or should

I say we are owned by, a senior Miniature Pinscher. I routinely take him outside every night so he can do his dog things. The sky at that time of night is beautiful, glistening with twinkling stars. That, moonlight, and a high-powered flashlight are the only illumination, no street or stop lights around.

Nothing eventful occurred until later that fall when, one night, an additional illumination was added. It was a beacon coming from that same mountainside. It had not been seen from the time we arrived until that fall. It was visible for three or four nights, then never again. From that time until this writing it has been visible maybe four to six times. Some suggest it is/was a beacon from an airport. If so, I would think it would be visible, if not nightly, much more frequently.

My nightly walks with the dog now are ones with an eye to the sky, a look over the shoulder, and that high-powered flashlight fully charged. One cannot be sure when visitors will be coming!

THE WHITE THING ON MEEKER TRAIL

*A*nonymous
      Cameron County

DURING A HIKE in the fall of 2019, I decided to hike the Ralph Seeley Meeker Run Trail in Cameron County. The day portion of the hike was typical enough, lots of birds and small animals to photograph. It was night when things got a little eerie.

It started with the sounds. At first I wrote them off as coyotes and the bugling of elks. It might have been that too, but something about it felt off. The noises had an ethereal feeling to them that made it hard to say which direction they were coming from. It felt like they were all around you.

The area is well-known locally for two reasons. First, because it was the former site of the Curtiss-Wright Nuclear Reactor. As I guess is typical of such places, there are rumors about animals being mutated by nuclear waste, although nothing was ever remotely proven of course.

The second is because a man named Mr. Meeker hid from a posse after being run out of a nearby town. He ended up living in a cave system for decades without being found as the cave system is concealed by rhododendron bushes. The man had doors on each end and even a chimney system to funnel out smoke from his fires without making his presence known.

The trail loops around three or so miles of forest, but if you venture off to explore the cave and rock system, it adds a couple miles on. I underestimated how long it would take and it was well past sunset by the time I was on my way back to my truck.

As I hiked, I heard a crashing through the underbrush. That wasn't unusual as it was the time of night everything from raccoons to deer are on the move, but I stopped and stood still to watch and see what was making the commotion. I had a lamp on my hat to light the trail in front of me, and I kept it fixed on the trail.

That's when I saw the white thing, a creature unlike anything I'd ever seen before. It was running full bore, mostly a blur, but I could tell it was on two legs. I'd estimate it stood six to seven feet in height. And when my light hit it, it shined so bright that it made me squint. It was moving so quick it was just a blur. There one second, gone the next.

It left a path of flattened brush in its path. I tried to look where it had fled, but by the time I got there, it was already gone. I thought about following that little path of smashed down weeds and saplings, but it was dark and I was alone and unarmed, so that seemed unwise.

To this day I don't know what I saw, but I know it wasn't any normal animal that belonged in those woods.

MY FIRST HOUSE

*B*y Frank W.
Pittsburgh Area

IN THE EARLY 2000s I bought my first house. I was fresh off a divorce and had a 5 year old daughter. My life was in chaos, but I wanted things to settle down. I thought having a home of my own, one I could stay in rather than moving from rental to rental, would help with that.

Moving in went as smooth as moves can go, and I finished up a few days after Thanksgiving. Even though I didn't feel overly celebratory, I wanted my daughter's first

Christmas in the house to be a happy one, so we went a little crazy with the decorations.

A few days after putting up the tree (a real one), I was awoken in the middle of the night to a muffled crash. My daughter was with my ex and I was alone, so I listened for a moment before exiting bed. When I didn't hear anything, I got up to explore.

I found the tree toppled onto its side, several of the ornaments broken, including the angel that went up top. That one was actually shattered beyond repair. I didn't think much of it. Just figured I didn't have it straight when I put it up and gravity caught up. I got it upright again and, the next day, went to buy replacement ornaments and a new angel.

The next week or so were normal. Then I got woken up by the sound of a door slamming, over and over again. Thankfully, I was alone when this happened too, as it freaked me out and I can only imagine how scared my girl would have been.

The door slamming continued as I got out of bed. I could tell it was coming from the first floor and I looked around for something I could use as a weapon in case there was an intruder. The one thing close by was a a candle, one of those in the glass jars. Not great, but better than nothing.

I crept down the stairs and made it about half way when the door slammed one more time, then the noises stopped. When I got to the first floor it was freezing cold even though the thermostat was sett around 65. All I could think was that someone had been opening the front door and letting cold air in, but when I checked, it was locked and dead bolted.

I decided to wait downstairs, to see if anything else happened or I heard anything. I sat back in the recliner and pulled an old quilt around me and waited. Sometime I fell asleep and woke around dawn. Nothing else had occurred.

I was never a big believer in ghosts, but I knew what I heard was real, so I went to my parent's house where I kept some guns and brought one of my old shotguns to the new place. I really thought someone was getting into my house somehow and I called a locksmith to change all the locks too.

After that, as Christmas approached, things just got weirder. My daughter came for a weekend and brought her cat. The whole weekend that cat stared into a downstairs bedroom. It barely took a break to eat and use the litter box. Every other second it just sat still as a statue and stared into that room, never going inside it though.

I'd bought my daughter some Christmas presents including one of those dolls that talks to you when you squeeze it or pull a string, I can't remember which. That present was wrapped and under the tree one night she was staying over.

In the middle of the night, I got up to go to the bathroom and heard the doll talk talking. I thought my daughter had snuck out of her room, gone downstairs, and opened her presents and I was a little annoyed as she knew better.

So, I marched down there, expecting to find her playing with the doll. But she wasn't there. And the doll was still in its box, wrapped up, yet chattering away. It went one for almost an hour, then stopped.

The worst was about a week before Christmas. The house had a basement and it sounded like World War 3 was going off down there one night. I mean, loud to the point where I was sure the whole basement would be destroyed. I heard glass breaking, things getting knocked over, banging, beating, stomping.

I almost called the cops, but with everything else that had happened, I decided to check it out myself first. I grabbed the shotgun and headed to the basement. Just as I opened the door, it went dead quiet.

I flipped on the light and went down the steps. Not a single things was broken or even moved. But I hadn't dreamt it. The noise had continued until I opened the door and had been so loud I could feel it shaking the floor.

That happened the next four nights. And I didn't get an hour of sleep. I was exhausted and nervous and flinching at every sound. I thought I was going to have to sell my house.

During that spell a neighbor saw me getting my mail and I must have looked like crap because she asked me if I was sick. I told her no and explained a little of what was going on. Turned out, she was Catholic and she said I should get the house blessed. I was a little religious, but had never thought things like that were real. She offered to call the priest at her church and I figured I didn't have anything to lose.

The next day the priest came out and

blessed the house. Nothing dramatic happened. Nothing at all, really. He just spritzed some water around and said some prayers and was on his way.

After that, nothing even remotely strange happened in the house. I still live there to this day and I'll be eternally grateful for that priest for allowing me to keep my home.

UNINVITED VISITOR

B y Scott Nightingale
Somerset

THIS IS an absolute true story and I can remember it as if it just happened last night even though it's been over forty years. On a quiet, snowy evening, I became a believer in ghosts.

My wife and I married in 1976 and secured a unit in a brick apartment building across from the Somerset Football field not long afterwards. The units were all brand new and families were moving in as soon as each was finished. Construction workers were still in the process of installing wiring, lighting, cabinets, painting, and carpeting when we were permitted to move in to our apartment.

Custer Realty managed the apartments, the manager graduating one year before me from the Somerset Area High School. It was explained to us that we could move in but there may be the need for construction workers to have access to our apartment when we weren't home and the manager told us that he had a pass key to our apartment.

He asked our permission to allow the workers to enter our dwelling, only if the construction workers needed inside to continue to finish other apartments. Of course, we had given our approval, so excited to move into our first home.

On the night of our experience, my wife Lisa and I had gone to bed in the bedroom facing the street. Light from the street lamps spilled through the thin window sheers, lighting up the room to the point where it wasn't much dimmer than daytime.

We weren't in bed long at all, with not a chance to even fall asleep, when my wife said, "Did you hear that?"

I nodded. "Yes".

She said, "It sounds like someone is trying to get into our apartment!"

I agreed and told her to be quiet and lay still. The noise we both heard was the sound of the doorknob being turned back and forth. I don't know why I didn't get up and investigate right away. I guess I thought it could be the apartment manager, but that late at night?

My wife was snuggled up close against me with her head on my right shoulder. We remained quiet and still. What I'm about to tell you is exactly what my wife saw and remembers to this day. We both saw the exact same thing.

With the room lit from the streetlight, a man walked ever so slowly into our bedroom. When he first entered the room, I whispered into my wife's ear, "There he is!"

As she shushed me, he continued in, stopping at the foot of our bed. Then he turned to face us.

We could not see through him, as you might expect with a ghost or spirit. He looked like a real man with a long coat and he wore what looked to be a Stetson hat. His arms hung at his sides in a non-threatening manner.

He stood there staring at us for maybe a

minute, but it felt much longer. He then slowly turned towards our bedroom door and exited as slowly as he entered. You could see from our bedroom door through the hallway, into the living room, and to the only door to our apartment on the second floor.

I allowed the man to get what I thought to be at the most, maybe ten feet from our bedroom when I jumped up and turned on the light as I moved to chase after him. I wanted to know who in the God's name was in the apartment.

But he was nowhere to be seen.

All through this, I could see the apartment door and it never opened. There was no new sound of a door opening or any other sound. We then slowly walked through the apartment calling out, "Who's here?" to no response.

My wife was right up against me following me through the apartment as I checked in closets, in the bathroom and behind things. Nothing! And we both saw the exact same thing and realized that it would have been impossible for him to get out as quick as I turned on the light.

I will always remember that evening. The strange thing is... after this, I don't remember my wife Lisa, or myself, being afraid that he may appear again. I don't think we actually brought it up often while living there. Over the years I told this story to many people, and the story doesn't change, because it is absolutely true!

In hindsight, I think we should have put it in the newspaper. This happened in Somerset and no one but our families know about it. It makes you think of how many other sightings happen and no one says anything. A Halloween season doesn't pass that I don't talk about the ghost of a man we witnessed together that night.

You can believe this because I am not one to make up stories like this. I've been living in the Greenville, South Carolina area since 1997 but do visit Somerset occasionally. When I do, I'm always tempted to stop by the apartment and as the current residents if they've ever seen the man in the Stetson Hat...

THE HOUSE AT THE TOP OF THE HILL

*B*y *Kelsey Andolina*
Johnstown

THE HOUSE that my parents bought in 1994, when I was two years old, was a real, living nightmare.

The main reason my parents settled on that particular house was because it was cheap. That was perfect for them as they were buying their first house together. They either neglected to ask why the price was so low, or perhaps certain history with this house or the land itself was not disclosed or even known. Regardless, I doubt they knew what horrors this house really held within its walls when they purchased it.

The physical house itself was very beautiful, but eerie. It sat on the top of a hill in a quiet, little neighborhood in Johnstown, Pennsylvania. The red brick, ranch-style house was built in 1945. It was completely surrounded by tall, thick pine trees. Because of this, not much natural light came into the house.

Although I was never physically hurt at my stay in that house, I was tormented psychologically for years by a spirit there. I only had to tolerate the house in the evenings and on some weekends, when I wasn't visiting my grandparents or my dad.

My mom and dad divorced when I was seven. My sadness and grief seemed to trigger a series of paranormal phenomena. It was as if I opened a door I could not shut. That was when the crazy dreams began and the insomnia followed. I found myself not sleeping because I knew if I did, I would dream terrible, painful things. These were matters that no child should have to experience. Many of these dreams I did not understand fully until much later in life.

My nights there were spent with my brother usually staying in my room at my request. I hated being alone at night. My mom or brother didn't mind because I had bunk beds. My nights were filled with *Three's Company*, *Cheers*, *Happy Days*, and fighting that feeling like someone was watching me. I distracted myself with television, but I didn't feel safe. There was a stench of heaviness that lingered there like a musty, old smell that you can't clear. I never told my mom about the dreams or the insomnia. Even at such a young age, I knew my mom was going through a lot and I did not want to burden her. Unfortunately, that house was all my mom had after the divorce.

I would have the same nightmares repeatedly. The dream that I refer to as "the man who leapt from the stairs" was one of them. It was always the same.

In it, I woke up as a man, alone in the morning, with some light actually entering my house. I got out of bed and walked down the hallway to the kitchen. The house felt slightly different, eerily quiet and empty. I hesitated when I reached the kitchen. That radiant light reached everywhere except the one corner of the kitchen where the basement stairs were located.

I walked very slowly to the stairs and

opened the basement door, revealing nothing but complete darkness. My toes curled around the top step and I rocked back and forth, like it was a game. I stared into the blackness, swaying.

Then, suddenly, something deep inside me, something dark and evil, made me leap. I jumped into the lightless basement, my stomach dropping like riding a steep, descending roller coaster. I would always wake up before I hit the bottom.

Years later, when revealing this dream to my brother, I can still remember the look on his face when I told him. Then, with the most serious tone I have ever heard him speak in, he told me that he also had this same, exact dream when we were in that house. The utter shock and the raw emotion he displayed convinced me he was being serious. It was comforting to have my experience validated, but it seemed to scare me more knowing it was all real.

After about a year of restless sleep and dreaming of being the man on the stairs, the next series of dreams began. I received one of those "My-size" dolls from my grandpa as a gift. She was only about an inch or two shorter than me when she stood. I always kept her in my closet when I wasn't playing with her, because I had a small room. This dream was also repetitive, and always the same.

In the dream, it was as if I woke up in my own bed. Something had startled me. I looked around my room for the source of the sound. Then, I heard the sound again. I spun around to find my closet door shaking forcefully. I approached it slowly and when my hand reached the door knob, the shaking stopped.

I opened the door slowly. There stood my doll, blinking and tilting her head, never taking her evil eyes off of me. She raised her hand, holding a large, sharp, butcher's knife. I tried to scream, but my cries were muffled like I was underwater. I tried to run away but it felt like my feet were in quicksand.

Then, the doll smiled wider and began stabbing me repeatedly in the stomach. The pain felt so real, ripping and cutting me deeply, almost like an intense burning sensation. It seemed to continue forever. As I sank to the floor, bleeding profusely, and giving up, I heard a deep, roaring laugh. It wasn't coming from the doll, but from behind her. I used the last bit of my strength to look up, into the closet. The laughter continued and now all I saw was glowing eyes staring at me in the shadowy closet.

It had been about a year of having this dream, nearly every night. One spring morning, like I did every morning, I opened my closet to get my school clothes. I noticed the doll wasn't there. I tore my closet apart, looking for her. She simply wasn't there.

I had not moved her for months. I was afraid to play with her after the dreams began. I searched the house, still in my pajamas. I cautiously crept into the unnaturally cold living room and there she was. She was sitting on my child-sized recliner chair.

I backed up slowly, without turning my back on her. I ran to my mom immediately to try to convince her we need to get rid of the doll. I didn't tell her about the dream, but she must have seen my fear. We put the doll outside for spring clean up that very morning with no questions asked.

Eventually, the dreams stopped. I don't know why or how. Those dreams will be locked in my memory forever. I truly believe that I was manipulated by a malevolent spirit through my dreams. I was fed upon spiritually, my fear being the fuel.

I have faced many obstacles in my life, but this was one of the hardest. I felt helpless, weak, and defeated for years because of this. As a child, I couldn't comprehend what was happening to me, only that it was something to be feared.

These events occurred between the years of 1999 – 2002. My mom, brother, and I moved out of the house in 2004. I am convinced that the close bond my brother and I share is what got me through it all. He was always there for me and we are still close to this day.

I feel like I did learn something from this experience; Love conquers all. I have never had nightmares like this since living there. I have lived in many houses. Nowhere ever came close to the heaviness, misery, dread, and horror that the house on the top of the hill gave me.

SHAFFER MOUNTAIN

*B*y Kelly Hofecker
Ogletown

I GREW UP IN OGLETOWN, a small community at the outskirts of Windber, just at the edge of Somerset and Bedford county. It's one of the small towns and scattered communities that sit on Shaffer Mountain, a rather wild and peaceful place that is a combination of private land, state forest, and land originally purchased by the Wilmore Coal companies to strip-mine, but instead were left to sit for the average person to use and enjoy. There is some lumber cutting going on currently, but nothing major, as it seems most agree that Shaffer Mountain is a special, wild place that deserves and needs to be left alone.

The underground streams are said to be the most pure water you will ever find, and fields of untended blackberries are ripe to be plucked. A heavy fog blankets and drapes across the mountains on all but the hottest of days. Sometimes you can even see it rolling in when the temperature changes from hot to cold.

The roads are mostly dirt and gravel, rife with potholes. Many of the roads have been closed, and some appear to lead nowhere in particular and without any signage. Some will tell you they have traversed these thick woods with an ATV and haven't seen or experienced anything in particular, and yet many an elder resident will tell you there's more to those mountains than meets the eye, and it would be wise to be back home before the sun sets.

There used to be a small lumber town on Shaffer Mountain called Crum, and it even still exists on some maps. A main road still carries the name, and one can find ruins of the old town if you know where to look. There are many rumors as to what became of the town, some more official than others.

The certified explanation is that the lumber mill became less profitable, the people grew sick of the harsh winters and sticky summers in the small mountain town, and left. Others however, sometimes including locals, tell of something more devious.

One story says the town was burned to the ground, the residents contracting something along the lines of smallpox or scarlet fever. The fire itself was set by the local government to keep the disease from spreading. I've heard some say they have seen the burned ruins, but there's no proof any of it is true. It's easy to believe, however, as those mountains are a magnet for the strange and unusual.

There was a book that detailed the history of Crum and surrounding areas - supposedly, even paranormal events. It was either located in Ogletown or the older town of Crum itself. However, there was only one copy of this book, and it was stolen. The only record of the history and events of that area completely wiped out by it's disappearance. It's an odd, perhaps unnerving action. What reason would someone have in taking this book, if not to hide something? And if so, what could that actually be?

The mountain is rife with supernatural tales, from simply odd behaviors of the residents, to full blown ghosts, and UFO sightings. Growing up, my parents would often come home from driving around the mountains in the evening and nights, along Crum Road and other roads nearby. Quite often they would come home with ghostly sightings that would bother my mother, a firm believer in the paranormal.

Sightings would include a man dressed in a flannel shirt, back to the road, arms to the side as he stood motionless under a tree. Recounting the story gives both of my parents a chill. Another story is of a black shuck, or black, ghostly dog running in front of them as they drove past the cemetery, disappearing before it even reached the tree-line. Wails and cries were heard from this cemetery once as my parents were higher up on a different road, needless to say they decided to get home a bit earlier that night.

Crum Cemetery, located near the original location of the town of Crum and on Crum Road, is perhaps the most popular local legend. Growing up, I heard quite a bit about the small, old, and oddly creepy rural cemetery in the mountains.

Once my parents took me on a ride to see it myself, and I caught sight of smaller, older tombstones coming into view from the bottom of the hill as we drove up. Many of the graves are simply rocks, wether replacements for previous stones or the only available marker for the family at the time. Back then, there were tall and sickly trees, at times hung with nooses. There would always be evidence of partying, like strewn beer cans, the place known to be a hotspot for the local youth.

There are stories of strange happenings at Crum Cemetery, some alluding to the idea that it was the living that urged the paranormal to a head to begin with. My sister used to party there, and we heard stories when she would return. There were the said nooses, animal skeletons, and occult materials like rings of candles. I remember hearing, very firmly, that cult activity had been discovered here, as had reports of the KKK. A friend of mine witnessed a white-hooded member dragging a deer through its grounds.

Some friends would give stories of red eyes

and sounds, odd, creepy feelings on Crum Road itself. Supposedly, if one were to park on the bridge leading to the cemetery, their car will not be able to restart. However said bridge has since been replaced, and it remains to be seen if the curse still remains.

Crum Cemetery has since been cleaned up, it's evil aura vanishing. One is lucky to get paranormal activity here now. However, one nearby place still retains it's prowess to terrify, and that's of the Murder Houses, otherwise known as The Dead Zone.

This is a legend that goes as far back as the 80's, when the original event occurred. A man killed his wife and daughter, the latter who he had been upset with after discovering she was going out with a boy. There are unconfirmed details, like him being a Vietnam veteran, and snapping due to PTSD, and using an axe to do the deed. Yet one fact is clear, he then went into his truck with a gun, and set it ablaze before committing suicide. My dad remembers seeing the pillar of smoke from the house that day, and driving down to witness the burnt-out truck itself, the air thick with an eeriness of what had transpired there.

I also know a friend of my parents who took the bumper from the truck to replace the one on his. I suppose you can say there's two types of people.

The original house was a marvel, it had a huge hand-made fireplace, a natural spring pool and extensive gardens. It became a party spot in the eighties just like Crum. Once my brother visited the place with a friend. When I brought up the houses at a campfire, they both questioned why I would want to go to such a messed-up place. He included tales of garden tools levitating in midair and being thrown, and red glowing eyes. His friend got wide-eyed at the mention of the place, telling us something had followed him home that night, and something had been in his room.

The main house had since been burned down by the local fire department. It had become dangerous and this was a way to keep anyone from hurting themselves. The energy and darkness in the place remains just as livid, however. The house next to it is also abandoned and in disrepair, and feels just as stained by the events of that day, and the houses down the mountain from there seem to be part of a road that no longer exists, they sit with no connection to the nearby towns, and seem to be accessible only by driving through the grass. Was the evil aura of this place so extreme, the neighboring families up and left? Or in some cases, even refused to drive past it?

Hauntings include the aforementioned red eyes, a feeling of an evil, demonic presence, physical attacks, spook-lights in the woods, and the lit cigarette of the murderer, seen near the large wooden gate at the top of the road. People have been chased on Roman Road, and it's said a man killed his brother on this road as well. Details, however, are sketchy. There are cairns in the woods as well, the origins of which are completely unknown to locals or tourists alike.

These aren't the only stories on the mountain. UFOs have been seen in the skies, and a friend of my parents was watching a light approach their bedroom window, then for it to vanish after they experienced missing time. There are a few bigfoot sightings nearby, and I personally have been subjected to heavy, bipedal footsteps in the woods. There have been other cryptid sightings as well, although they are fewer and far between.

Above all, the pull this place has is

intoxicating. It's not just that the woods are quiet, serene and private. There's something in the air and earth that lingers, that calls you back to unravel its mysteries again and again. It is doubtful, however, that we will uncover them anytime soon.

GHOSTLY SHEET

 *y Les Griffith*
Boswell

I HAVE a true story to tell you...

A ghost story...

I was six-years-old at the time. My mom was married for the second time and we lived with my stepdad in Boswell, PA.

We'd spent the day visiting my grandma in Friedens. Around evening, the grown-ups decided it was time to head home. Instead of taking the highway, my stepdad decided on taking the back way home to Boswell.

The drive was typical enough until, suddenly, a huge white sheet covered the whole road in front of the car. It was so high up it touched the telephone wires and stretched for yards off the road before disappearing into the woods.

I sat, frozen in the back seat, peering through the windshield as my stepdad slammed on the breaks. As soon as the car stopped and he threw open the door, the sheet vanished. There was no evidence it had ever been there, but all of us had seen it.

Afterward, we reported it to the police in Boswell. They thought we were nuts and didn't do anything. But I seen what I saw and will never forget it as long as I live...

BIGFOOT ON THE MOUNTAIN

*B*y *Bobbi*
Uniontown Area

OUR CAMP WAS LOCATED in Southwestern, PA, on the mountain above Uniontown. This was the summer of '83 and I had just turned 15.

It was a scorching hot afternoon and my brother, sister, nephew, a kid from the campground, and I were playing kickball. My nephew kicked the ball and I chased after it. The field was littered with rocks, so running wasn't very easy and I was trying not to trip when my brother yelled, "*Stop!*" So, I did.

Growing up in and around the woods we

were taught, when someone says *stop* you stop. Actually, you freeze in place because you might be about to step on a poisonous snake. So, I'm looking around at the ground trying to figure out if I'm about to get bit, when my brother tells me to look up at the tree line. I did, but to this day I don't know what I saw.

It was tall, about eight and half feet. Covered in dark matted hair. And it stunk! It smelled like rotting meat, sewage, and musty, moldy, damp dirt. The creature was about a hundred and fifty feet from us, and it didn't move.

It stood there, just looking at us. I'll never forget how it got so quiet. The birds, which had been singing away, stopped. All of us couldn't make a peep. The only sound were the flies buzzing. So many flies.

We stared for what felt like an eternity, then my brother told me to walk back to him. I did, but I walked backwards, afraid to take my eyes off that huge thing standing in the tree-line - watching us. Eventually the creature turned away, stomping through the brush toward a slate dump.

When I got back to the group, we had no interest in continuing the game. We ran back to camp, and put a fire in the two wheels we used as a fire pit. We usually cut the slabs of wood into six pieces, but that day we used half or full size. We wanted it as big as we could get it.

When my folks got back from town, they pulled in and saw flames about twenty feet in the air. I was sitting there, gripping my dad's .22 like it was glued to my hands. First words out of my dad's mouth was, "Why are you touching the gun and why is the fire so big?"

So, we told him what happened.

He said to me, "Come on. Let's go see what we can find."

Dad grabbed his deer rifle and let me keep the .22 as we walked over to where we had seen the creature. The smell still lingered, but wasn't as strong. You could see where the brush was broke off and flattened, proof something big had walked through it .

We followed its trail to the top of the slate dump. There, you could see chunks of slate kicked aside, brushed out of the way of the creature. We kept walking.

We followed the trail deeper into the woods, but it eventually faded out. Dad said we better get back because mom would have supper ready, so we turned and returned to camp.

After supper, Dad said he was going to go scout around again, but he was going through the back end of the camp area. He told me to stay back since it was getting dark.

He was gone less than fifteen minutes before he burst back into came, pulling mom aside and whispering something to her, keeping his voice low so the rest of us couldn't hear. I heard mom say, "We'll have to wait until morning to pack up. It's too dark now."

Dad came to me and told me to help him set fires all around our camp. We built them about five feet apart. I asked him why we was doing this and he said to keep things away and so we could see better.

He and I sat up all night long and kept watch over the camp . We didn't see or hear anything but, come daylight, we packed up camp and never went back.

Over the years I asked my dad what he'd seen, but he'd never answer me. My dad was a big, tough man and wasn't easily spooked, but whatever he saw made him not want to camp there again.

Shortly before he passed away I asked him

one last time what he saw. He looked at me and said, "You know what I seen, now just never mind talking about it."

I can't say for a hundred percent that what I saw was a bigfoot, but I don't know what else it could have been.

THE HAUNTED APARTMENT

B y Deborah Vick
Johnstown

NEARLY 60 YEARS ago my best friend's sister
and two of her friends decided they were ready
to live on their own, so they rented their first
apartment. It wasn't anything fancy, but it was
affordable and in what was a pretty safe
Johnstown neighborhood at the time.

The apartment was located in a big, old
house - the kind they show in spooky movies
with lightning flashes to illuminate it. It was
dark and creepy, even in the daylight. The
house had been split into two units, one
apartment on the ground floor, another on the

second story and it was the upper residence where the friends lived.

Through donations from friends and family they cobbled together furniture and decorations and, while it wasn't much, it was a home of their own. The girls shared a kitchen and bath, while each had their own bedroom. It was the freedom they all so coveted.

But, a few weeks into their stay, odd things began to occur. The girl who was sleeping in the room with attic access complained about hearing frequent creaking noises coming from above. The others thought she was imagining it, but to keep her happy they swapped her bedroom and the living room so she was out of that room. Things calmed down for a while, until they all started to hear the creaking noise while sitting in the living room.

To go along with the odd noises, one of the girls started dreaming about a little boy in the house and she became so scared she moved out and moved home. Now there were just two of them. Since my friend's sister usually worked until after nine at night, the other girl was often spending her evenings alone in the apartment and it didn't take long until she too became so unnerved that she decided to move back home.

My friend's sister wasn't any less spooked than the others, but she was determined not to move back home, so she talked my friend and I into coming over and staying with her. We just kind of rolled our eyes at stories about the noises in the attic and strange dreams, thinking there was a simple explanation. Plus, the apartment was closer to our school so our moms said it was okay and we moved in.

At first it was kind of cool living there, but then we began hearing things too and started thinking maybe they weren't crazy after all. We closed and locked the room with the door to the attic and kept the radio or TV on all the time when we were home.

But, when it got quiet, you could still hear a repetitive creak-creak coming from above that sounded like someone rocking in an old rocker. Pretty soon we were getting spooked too and my friend and I would stay in town or at another friend's house and wait for her sister to get there so we were never there by ourselves. We mentioned moving home, but she begged us to stay and we felt guilty about leaving her. So we stayed.

By this time we were all sleeping in one room and all in the same bed. One night it seemed the creaking got louder than usual and we also heard what sounded like someone walking around up there. Laying in bed, afraid to leave the room, we convinced ourselves someone or something was up in the attic.

We considered rats or squirrels. Maybe even a raccoon could explain away the sounds. But, we weren't that convinced and of course we weren't brave enough to go look ourselves, so we called the police. They showed up and actually went into the attic, shining flashlights around while we peaked up the stairs, waiting for something horrible to occur. But nothing did.

As they came back down, we could tell they were annoyed because they stomped straight to the exit, telling us they hadn't seen anything. But, to us, they looked in too big a hurry to get out of there, so we decided it was time for us to go too.

It was around 2am on a frigid, snowy night, but we took off and walked from Kernville to Prospect. A few days later we needed to go back and get our clothes. As we were heading into the house, an old lady across the alley hollered at us. She said she wasn't being nibby, but she saw the police there the other night and then saw us leave and had been concerned about us.

We told her about what had been going on, the noises, the dreams, the sense of unease, and she listened. Then she said she needed to tell us a story.

She said she didn't want to scare us, but she'd lived in her house since she was a young child and back then the family that lived in our house had a son who was what they then called retarded. Sadly, people would isolate these children from the rest of the family and the little boy always seemed to be in the attic and would sit in a rocking chair by the little window and wave to people outside.

Then she told us that the boy had been sitting in that rocker, looking out the window, when he died.

After hearing her story, we were pretty sure we had our answer about who was in the attic. We went in and grabbed our clothes and personal things and got out in a hurry. Several days later her brother in law and some friends went and got the furniture. She told the landlord he could sue her for breaking the lease if he wanted, but she was not going to live in that apartment again for love nor money.

Maybe we were all young girls with a flare for the dramatic or maybe there really was a lonely little boy living in that attic. I don't know...

But I do know I still get goosebumps when I hear the creak-creak, creak-creak, creak-creak of an old rocking chair.

HAUNTED HIKE ON WOPSY MOUNTAIN

*B*y Wanda Chambliss
Altoona

ONE SPRING, after the snow finally got around
to melting off, my best friend and I decided to
do a weekend hike and camp on Wopsononock
Mountain in Altoona. Or, as anyone from that
area calls it, Wopsy Mountain.

We'd heard that the mountain was haunted
and that was part of the appeal for me. That
stuff fascinates me. Plus, it's a beautiful
location so, even without any ghosts, it was
bound to be a nice weekend.

We were hiking a trail off Lookout Road
and made camp for the night. I'd scrabbled

together some sticks and twigs which my friend used to start a campfire. We roasted a couple hot dogs and just enjoyed the scenery and nature. It was a fine evening.

I woke up around midnight having to pee. That's the worst part about camping. So I fumbled around in the tent until I found a flashlight and the roll of toilet paper we'd brought, then headed into the night.

I was squatting behind a tree and, thank goodness I had my pants down, when I saw what I believe to be a ghost. A white shape, probably four feet high, drifted through the trees. It looked like a small, floating cloud bank.

But it had substance to it. When it brushed by a small sapling, the thin, little branches on the sapling moved just like someone had pushed it aside with their fingers.

I lost sight of it as it moved through the trees and hurried to finish my business as quick as possible. But, by the time I was zipped up and went exploring, it was gone.

Nothing else happened during the weekend, but afterward I did some reading and found out about the "white lady of Wopsy Mountain" and I believe that's what I saw.

The story behind her is simple enough. A

newly married couple, way back in the horse and buggy days, was leaving their home at the top of Wopsy Mountain. The road was very steep and the wagon picked up too much speed and they crashed. Both were thrown from the wagon and killed.

The wife's body was found, but the husband's never was. They say the wife still roams the mountain, searching for her lost husband, and that's she'll continue to look until his remains are found.

I've been back a few times since then but haven't been lucky enough to see her again. Who knows, maybe she finally found him.

MOM'S UFO

$\mathcal{B}$*y Heidi Hampe*
Somerset

WHEN I WAS A LITTLE GIRL, my mother's encounter with a UFO intrigued me and spurred my curiosity of the unknown. I would ask her to tell me about it over and over again.

My grandmother, Margaret, an immigrant from Scotland, married my grandfather, Floyd, in 1933. They moved to Somerset where they lived on a small farm at the bottom of Briar Patch Road. There they raised six children including my mother, Marian, who was the youngest of the six. Grandma never learned to drive, as she said she had enough kids to take her where she wanted to go. Life on the farm was simple and good.

On a warm summer evening in 1979 just after sunset Margaret, then age 69, along with Marian, age 22, loaded up their '72 Ford Pinto with laundry and headed up Briar Patch road toward the laundromat. Margaret didn't have a washer and dryer and six kids make a lot of dirty laundry. Winding up the one lane road in a leisurely fashion, they chatted and laughed and enjoyed the warm evening breeze through the rolled down windows; Pinto's did not have air conditioning.

As they rounded the corner by Old Man Johnson's farm, something in the air didn't feel quite right. Suddenly, in an instant there it was... something strange and enormous up to the left of the car, right over Johnson's pond. There was no sound at all, just an oblong object, about the size of a mobile home, hovering silently over the water.

Neither of them spoke as they watched something unfold in front of them which their minds could barely grasp. The object was black and gray, solid and dome-shaped, tapering off to both sides.

On each side was a light; a round red one

on the left side and a green blinking one on the right. As they watched, awestruck, spheres of white light began to drop, one after the other, from the bottom of the object. These balls of light dissipated just before they hit the water in Old Man Johnson's pond. All the while there was no sound at all. Whatever was powering the object and ejecting the white balls was using a silent energy.

They never stopped the car, just drove slowly past the object while it completed it's unknown mission. Neither of them spoke for a long while. Later, my mom timidly asked my grandma, "Did you see what I saw?"

"Yes," was all she said. The chatting was over; neither spoke much for the rest of the trip.

Dome shaped objects with flashing lights ejecting balls of light have been reported all over the world for some time. The type of sighting they witnessed is a common one in the UFO world, but there is nothing common about it when you see it for yourself, up close. Today, my mom wonders why they didn't stop the car and watch the entire spectacle. Perhaps it's best they just kept on driving.

GHOST HOUSE

*B*y Renee L. Barnes
Western PA

MANY YEARS ago my friend Winnie and her son Mich moved into a isolated farm house. It was perfect for them as they had a menagerie of pets, everything including dog, goats, and horses. It seemed like a dream come true, but ended up being a nightmare.

Shortly after they returned home, I made my first visit to their new home. It had been years since we'd seen each other in person and we spent most of the visit catching up.

As Winnie showed me around, I greeted the animals, a love we both shared. I also met

Mich for the first time. He had special needs and was wary of my presence, but the boy was polite and welcoming after I introduced myself.

Winnie mentioned feeling of heaviness in the house and I felt it too, but we wrote it off as old wiring. Then she showed me a cell phone pic she had snapped of a rocking chair. There was a large, blurry spot in the center, so obvious it was almost hard to see through. Still, it wasn't something we thought too much about at the time.

The strange phenomena increased as time passed. Unusual noises, odd feelings. One night Winnie called me in a panic to tell me that her gas stove kept lighting itself at all hours of the day. It happened so often that she ended up disconnecting the stove to prevent a possible fire.

All of this really had me interested and worried and I began digging in to the history of the farmhouse. I learned about a family named Prunty who had lived there in the 1800s. They were Polish and the father was controlling and stern. The mother made potions and home remedies, but eventually the father grew weary of her interacting with others and kept the family confined in the house.

One day, Mich came to us and told us about seeing small children playing in the house. That lined up with my research on the Prunty family who had several of their own.

More odd and unexplainable things kept happening. A stained glass cross fell off the wall and shattered. Winnie's goats began acting strangely and the baby goats passed away. Objects disappeared, only to reappear in other rooms.

One day, while I was visiting, Winnie's car began to roll down the driveway! She had to sprint after it, dive inside, and slam on the brakes before it crashed into the cornfields.

Winnie and Mich were so scared that they called their local clergyman, Pastor Joe, to come over and bless the house. As he climbed the steps to the second floor, he said he felt like something enormously strong was pushing against him, trying to prevent him from continuing. He made it to the top, but was so tired he could barely breathe and he felt like something unwelcome was trying to get inside his head.

Pastor Joe retreated to the kitchen where he was so exhausted he collapsed onto his knees. After a break to gather himself, he forced his way though the house, blessing it with prayers and holy water. He reassured Winnie that he would return if she needed his help again.

Later that night Winnie heard more sounds coming from he second story - footsteps and singing. She initially thought it was Mich and went to look for him. But, she found Mich in his room and the sounds still went on.

Winnie called Pastor Joe again and told him of the continued goings on. He was disappointed and said he would return with a priest.

The next day I went to Winnie's house with my camera and a voice recorder. We took photos filled with orbs and also got a photo of the bathroom mirror where the reflection was full of odd geometric shapes and something that looked like an ornately written letter G.

We lost track of the strange things that happened. One time a dog was chewing on a toy when the toy flew out of its mouth like something had jerked it away. Winnie also began seeing apparitions of a little girl, strolling through the house at all times of the day and night and Mich also kept seeing ghost children.

They began seeing figures in the trees around the property and there were more occurrences of her car slipping out of gear and rolling down the drive. One time it almost ran over some of the remaining goats! Winnie heard voices whispering in her ear but couldn't make out the words as they were in another language. Even the animals seem scared, constantly trembling and afraid to go into their barn.

I saw and heard these things myself, as did other visitors to the house. Winnie became so upset and scared that he blood pressure began to soar out of control and she had to go on medicine. Mich was so terrified that he came to live with me temporarily.

I helped them look fora new home, but all their animals made it hard to find a place. After almost endless searching, we found a new home. I helped Winnie move, a laborious task, but a necessary one. Whatever was on that farmhouse property wanted her out and I knew, if Winnie didn't escape, she'd die there. Maybe not from the ghosts, but from the physical and emotional toll it was taking on her.

With the move almost finished, Winnie returned one day to the farmhouse to get her last few belongings. As she drove up to the house, her car stopped. It didn't stall or shut off, but it stopped moving forward like there was an invisible impediment. Winnie hit the gas, but the car would not move forward. She put it in reverse and it worked fine. That was enough! She made a u-turn, headed back up the driveway, and never returned.

We later learned that a worker had gone to the house afterward, to check the house's plumbing and wiring to ensure everything was working as they prepared to rent the house again. While there he began to feel sick. Just a few hours later, he died of a massive heart attack.

So much more happened, it would take a whole book to tell it all, but hopefully I was able to capture the spirit of the incidents at the ghost house. I hope you enjoyed reading this. I know those of us who lived it sure are believers now! But most of all, remember God controls everything in our lives, and He is the ultimate one to determine our fates.

OUR LITTLE SPIRIT CHILDREN

B y Gidget Brooks
Pottstown

I HAVE ALWAYS BEEN interested in the unexplained and paranormal. Ghost stories intrigued me. Do I believe in UFO's? Of course I do! I love a good conspiracy theory, and will read about it all night long. Bigfoot, well maybe, I would never say never. But I don't think you ever TRULY believe until you have an experience of your own.

I had quite a few experiences that I had chalked up to coincidence, or just weird things that went on, but never really had a definitive "paranormal" experience until my son was born. I had him later in life, and I was so excited to finally have the child I had always wanted. He was, and still is the light of my life.

Several *coincidences* happened around and after his birth, but it wasn't until he was two that I had my first true and identifiable paranormal experience.

We lived in a small apartment in Pottstown, Pa. My son had just transitioned from a crib to a toddler bed. He was very good about not getting out of bed unless he called us first. It was a few months after he moved into his "big boy bed", and we were all sound asleep. It was about 1 am, and I woke up thinking I had heard him running through the apartment.

I was not an exceptionally light sleeper, but like most moms, I was tuned into listening for my son. I listened for a short while and, upon not hearing anything else, went back to sleep. Shortly after that, I was awakened again by the sound of little feet running through the apartment.

In our apartment, you could go in a circle from the kitchen, through the dining room, into the living room and into the hall where the bedrooms were, and back to the kitchen. While I was trying to decide if I should get up and put him back to bed or if he would just return to bed on his own, I heard the pitter patter of little feet take off again for another lap.

This time I was sure I was not dreaming and this being the third time I had heard those little feet smacking across the tile floor, I figured I better get up and try to get him back to sleep. As I walked out of my bedroom, I called out to him to get back to bed, as I hadn't heard the steps run back into his room this time.

Needless to say, I was startled when I heard him answer from his room. He said in an excited voice, "Mommy did you see them?"

I flipped the light on and there he sat on the edge of his "big boy" bed, wide awake. Not knowing what he was talking about, and more than a bit confused I asked, "Who?"

He said "The kids! Didn't you see them? They just ran into the kitchen."

Not knowing what to think, I asked, "What kids?"

He replied "The kids that came to play with me."

144

Looking around, I saw toys laying all over the floor. It was always our routine to put all the toys away before bedtime, so this was not normal for our household.

He noticed me staring at the toys and said "Mommy, the kids got them out, they just wanted to play. I know I am not allowed out of bed at night, so I just watched them from here."

I immediately went through the whole apartment looking for children that must have somehow gotten in our locked and childproofed door. Knowing that by all sound logic, there couldn't be any extra children in the apartment. But also seeing that my son was so proud that he didn't break the rules and get out of bed when he wasn't supposed to.

Well, needless to say, there were no other children there. At this point I wasn't quite sure what to do. I know that I had heard those footsteps, not once but three times. My son was not the kind of child to make up stories and had not learned the art of lying yet, so that didn't seem like an explanation either. And, he was so excited to have kids there to play with. Kids can't fake that kind of excitement.

I wasn't afraid. After all, it was just little kids. I was very intrigued, but didn't know what kind of explanation to give my son. After a few minutes of talking with him I decided on what seemed to be my best plan of action. I announced in a fake stern voice that it was past all little kids' bedtime and we must pick up the toys and get everyone back into bed. I put the toys away, I told his new friends that they needed to go home and get back into bed. I tucked my son back into his bed, gave good night kisses again and turned out the light.

As I left the room, I said in my best *Mommy means it* voice, "That means everyone stays in bed and goes to sleep." Then, I went back to my room. I sat on the edge of the bed for a few minutes just listening to my son breathe through the baby monitor, only just realizing that I hadn't even woke his father up.

I called to him, shook him, and finally roused him from his deep sleep. I told him all that had just happened. As he listened, he had a very odd, confused expression on his face. When I finished, he said that on several nights he had thought he heard little footsteps running through the apartment. He'd even got out of bed to tuck our son back in, but every time when he went into his room he found him sound asleep.

He assumed it was a dream - a dream that had happened several different nights. He said he didn't mention it because he felt embarrassed, but that now it made more sense.

Over the next day or two, I worked little questions into conversations with my son. I asked how many kids there were and he said two, a boy and a girl. I asked why they came to our apartment at night and he said to play with him because he didn't have brothers or sisters to play with. He also said they came at night because they didn't think I would like it if they came during the day when we had things to do. I asked who they were and if he knew their names. He said they never said their names, but they kept watching for their uncle.

After that, I heard the footsteps several more times. I usually just called out and said, it is bedtime, all little kids must get back into bed and go to sleep. And the footsteps would end.

Over the next seven years those little children made sure I didn't forget them in a number of different ways. I had heard one of them speak, found toys out of the toy box downstairs when I knew that we had put them all away before going to bed, found favorite outfits that were outgrown and that we had packed away in the attic laid out on the bed in the morning, and many other signs that those children were still with us during that time.

But eventually, the sounds stopped. Strangely, I missed the things the children did to remind me of their presence

All of this intensified my interest in the paranormal, and I began reading and researching everything I could get my hands on. "Sherry", a very close friend of mine also had the same interests, but for different reasons, and we both looked into many different aspects of paranormal.

Sherry met a psychic she said was very good. I wasn't sure if I even believed in psychics, so I decided I wasn't going to give her any info to go on, no clues that she could figure out generalities with and make them sound good. Nothing. I went in with my best poker face on. She said first that my grandmother was there. Ok, good guess. She had a 50/50 chance my grandmother had passed. Her next comment was, "The kids are here too."

I just sat there, not saying a word. She continued, "The little boy and girl that lived with you. They say they liked it at your house. They feel safe there."

I said I wasn't sure I knew who she was talking about. She replied, "The ones that run through your apartment and wake you up."

I was speechless and had tears streaming down my face and didn't even know why. She continued and said, "I know you have met their uncle, he was at your front door and startled you."

That made me recall a night when I'd seen an old man with a yellow raincoat on, standing at my door. I was shocked, as my porch was enclosed and the door to it was always locked in the evening. As a million thoughts of what to do went through my head, he was just gone. I thought it was weird, but chalked it up to just one of those things, and went on about my business. But somehow I knew now who it was now.

The psychic said that, a long time ago the uncle was watching the children play near a lake. A terrible storm blew in and both children fell into the lake and had drowned. The uncle, who was terribly guilt ridden, had passed away sometime after and had been watching over them ever since. She said that they had latched onto my son and wanted to watch over him so that nothing bad happened to him.

I sat there in total disbelief. There was no way she could have known any of the details she had told me. She said that she knew I was having a hard time understanding how she could know all of this, and she was right. I asked her if all of this is true, then where did the children go.

She seemed to be listening to someone I could not hear. She then replied, "The children said your son has a man that watches over him now."

Now the tears were really coming. My son's father had passed away right around the time that the children seemed to have gone away. She went on to give me many details of my life with names and specific details.

Several years later I had another meeting with this psychic. Out of the blue, she said there are two children here that want you to know they are fine. I asked if she knew who they were, and she said no, but the little girl smiled and said that you know who they are. I did. I asked where they have been, to which she replied that they have gone to the other side, your son will be ok now with his new guardian angel. And that was the last we have heard of the two little children that apparently stayed with us for seven years.

My son doesn't really remember the children, although he has heard this story many times. But I am thankful that they watched over him when they did.

DAD'S AFTERSHAVE

*B*y Maria Cumming
Altoona

MY FATHER DIED in November of 1982 when I was 8. I was an only child and I was daddy's girl. His death wasn't sudden, as he'd been diagnosed with cancer in June.

Even at an early age I knew the permanency of death. My great grandmother died a year prior to his passing and my grandmother passed away in June of 1982.

I was in school the morning my dad. I was using the restroom and, when I turned to open the stall door, I caught a whiff of Aqua Velva.

For those who don't know, Aqua Velva was

a popular aftershave in the 70s and 80s and it has a very distinct odor. It was also the aftershave my dad wore and I loved the smell of his cheeks!

So, when I caught that distinct odor, I was expecting to see him outside the girls' bathroom. I walked out and didn't see him. So, I walked down the hallway, hoping he was looking for me.

When I finally went back to class, my teacher called me up to her desk scolded me for being gone for about 15 minutes. She said, "It is 9:55, you left here at 9:40."

I went back to my desk and tried to focus on school. I kept thinking about smelling that after shave.

At 10:30 my mom came to the classroom and my teacher went out to speak with her. After a while my teacher came in and quietly got my coat and lunchbox and walked me out into the hallway.

I didn't say anything to my mom right away, but when we got to the stairway landing, I asked if daddy had died. She turned and stooped down to my eye level. With tears in her eyes, she quietly said, yes. I asked her when he died. And she replied at 9:45.

I truly believe that he wanted to let me know that he was there in that bathroom and it was his time to go. Every so often I will catch a whiff of Aqua Velva for just a slight second and I like to think that it's dad checking in on me.

THE BEAST ON BROWN ROAD

B *y Lee Varner*
Somerset County

I'VE NEVER BELIEVED in ghosts or aliens or creatures like bigfoot. The subject never even interested me. All I believed was what I saw with my own two eyes. Until the fall of 2008.

The exact date has slipped from my mind, but it was around the middle of November, before Thanksgiving. The time change had already passed by, which meant it was dark a little after 5pm. Those short days always made it hard to get anything accomplished, so by the time I was finished with work and made a quick stop at the grocery store, I felt like the day was already gone.

I was on my way home, heading toward the southern part of the county, and taking my usual course. One of the many rural, two-lane country roads I took was Brown Road.

Brown was typical of roads in that area. Narrow, winding, plenty of hills and dips. There were few houses and no street lights of any kind. All that lit up the land was the moon and the headlights of my Sportage.

Thick woods occupied the area on either side of Brown Road and I made a point to be alert, especially that time of year and that time of day. Because, as those in the rural Pennsylvania know, that's prime time for deer to be running.

I can't recall how many times I missed clipping a whitetail by less than a few feet. The things seem to appear out of thin air, bouncing across the road, oblivious to the two tons of steel threatening to flatten them.

I saw plenty of other wildlife on that road over the years. Raccoons, possums, a few turkeys, and porcupines. I even saw a mama bear and three cubs many a year back.

But I'd never seen anything like what crossed ahead of me that November night.

As I rounded one of the curves, what I can only describe as a beast lumbered out from a copse of pines and stepped right in front of me. My headlights hit it and gave me a good look. Maybe too good.

This beast stood on two legs, covered head to toe with dense, muddy brown fur. Its yellow eyes blazed as they caught the reflection of my headlights and its head snapped to attention as it looked right back at me.

The face was like that of a hound, a long muzzle and black nose. I couldn't make out any ears, but the head definitely made me think of a canine. Its front legs hung at its side, but I didn't get a good look at the hands or feet, or whatever was at the end of those appendages. I'd estimate it as being between five and six feet in height.

I know this will sound insane, but my first thought was - *I'm looking at a werewolf.* Not because I believed in such nonsense, but because it reminded me of one of those creatures in the movies. It didn't howl at the moon or bare its fangs or anything like that. It simply loped away, to the opposite side of the road. As it moved away from me, I saw a long tail, probably two feet in length and bushy like a fox's tail. Then, it vanished in the cover of the trees.

I stared for a moment, too shocked to comprehend what I'd seen. I stared at that spot in the trees where it slipped away, wonder if it might return - and hoping it wouldn't. I didn't stick around long though, stomping down the pedal and leaving a bit of rubber on the road as I made my own hasty retreat.

It took me years before I told anyone about this experience. What eventually led to me breaking my silence was a TV show on Native American mythology in which they mentioned "dogmen." The sketches they showed of such creatures looked almost exactly like what I saw that night on Brown Road.

I've driven down Brown hundreds, maybe thousands, of times since then and never saw the creature again. But I know it was there that night. And a part of me knows it's still out there.

AFTERWORD

I hope you've enjoyed Pennsylvania's Unexplained Mysteries! If you've had any experiences you would like to share, please visit me on the web at www.TonyUrbanAuthor.com

Additionally, if you enjoyed this book then I know you will LOVE "Pennsylvania's Most Haunted Places." Jam-packed with details and personal encounters at over 50 of the most haunted places in the state, the book will be released on October 1, 2022. You can preorder the ebook now and print versions will be available in October.

Until next time, stay scared!

Tony Urban

Also by Tony Urban
> Her Deadly Homecoming
> Within the Woods
> Hell on Earth

Made in the USA
Las Vegas, NV
25 October 2023

79646477R00094